W9-DFR-190

A Pocket Book for Industrial Archaeologists

A Pocket Book
for
Industrial Archaeologists

Kenneth Hudson

John Baker · London

T
37
H83

First published 1976
John Baker (Publishers) Ltd
35 Bedford Row, London WC1R 4JH

© John Baker (Publishers) Ltd

ISBN 0 212 97018 6

Printed and bound in Great Britain by
Morrison and Gibb Ltd, London and Edinburgh

Contents

Illustrations

Introduction

There are two possible reasons for taking an active interest in industrial archaeology. One is the hope of adding something to the store of knowledge about our industrial past, and the other is the wish to improve one's personal education by developing a better understanding of how our ancestors worked and supported themselves and their families, and of the changes in technology to which people had to adapt themselves, generation by generation.

During the past twenty years, what still remains of yesterday's industry and transport has been pretty thoroughly located and sifted by a remarkably varied collection of people, some professionals, but a great many more amateurs, carrying out the work in their spare time. As a result of their efforts, there are probably very few machines, factory buildings, railway and canal relics and mills surviving from the eighteenth and nineteenth centuries which have not been located, photographed and described. Some examples must certainly have been overlooked, but in general one could say that the first wave of interest in industrial archaeology has completed its main task – to record and, in some cases, to preserve the monuments of the age of steam. In museums and on their original sites, a great deal of historically important material has been preserved for future generations to see and study, and the British public at all levels has been made aware that steam engines and flour mills, and slate quarries, and chainmaking workshops are as respectable or interesting and as tourist-worthy as castles, cathedrals and country houses. When one thinks of the very different situation in 1950, this represents a great triumph. The industrial archaeologists can fairly claim to have broadened both historical awareness and the definition of history.

'Industrial archaeologists' is, however, a portmanteau term, which covers an extraordinary range of people. There have been economic historians, social historians, engineers, geographers, art historians and many other kinds of specialists in academic posts. To them one must add a rich assortment of professional people -- architects, teachers, doctors and so on – and another equally wide-ranging group, whose skills are mainly practical. And there have been thousands more who fall into no particular category, but who have enjoyed industrial archaeology as a hobby. Most of them, but by no means all, have attached themselves to some sort of group. Some have found ways of publishing reports of their findings. Others have been content to make their contributions more or less anonymously, and to allow their work to be absorbed into the total effort of the group to which they belong. They have been cleaners and painters of machinery, diggers-out of silted up canals, finders and interviewers of old people with memories of how a job used to be done, payers of subscriptions, faithful attenders at lectures and demonstrations, and makers of tea. They can all fairly claim to have been members of that very British development, the industrial archaeology movement. The blend of the academics' passion for shape, theory, classification and higher degrees and the amateurs' impatience with scholarly 'disciplines' and demands to see human activity as a whole has produced excellent results. A democratic willingness to respect other people's interests has been one of the most attractive and fruitful aspects of industrial archaeology.

But time, inevitably and fortunately, moves on and industrial archaeologists, if they are not simply to fossilise into a national federation of Old Boys' Clubs, are finding themselves obliged to redefine their objectives in terms of the 1970s and 1980s. In Section One, a personal view of what these objectives should be is given. At this point, it seems only necessary to say, with all possible emphasis, that the opportunities of the next twenty years are just as great as those which the pioneers of the 1950s and 1960s tried to tackle, that the problems, for reasons which will be explained, are likely to be rather greater and that the social and political implications of not only industrial archaeology but of all archaeology are going to be considered increasingly important. By 1980 it will have become more difficult, if not actually disreputable and reactionary, to define industrial archaeology in terms of objects and technical processes. Machinery will be thought of and described with a much more highly developed conscious-ness of the men and women who used it, earned a living from it and, all too frequently, suffered from it.

This Pocket Book has been written in the strong hope that what might be called the humanisation of industrial archaeo-logy is coming sooner, rather than later. It has been planned especially to meet the needs of people whose interest in industrial archaeology is comparatively recent and who want to apply their energies in the most effective and satisfying way. The title emphasises the aim – to provide the kind of guide and reference book that can be easily slipped into the pocket and consulted when need or inclination arises. It is a series of signposts, not a textbook.

There are as many reasons for taking up industrial archaeo-logy as for taking up golf and no two people are motivated in quite the same way. For some, the appeal is that of the treasure-hunt – using a succession of clues to discover for-gotten or concealed objects. For others, there is the pleasure and stimulus of meeting other people with similar enthusiasms and obsessions; the liberation of learning about history through tangible, visible things, rather than books; the opportunity to hunt out industrial veterans in retirement and to persuade them to reminisce about their work; the new field of activity for photography and drawing.

The great majority of industrial archaeologists carry out their self-appointed tasks within twenty miles of where they live. With few exceptions, this is a special kind of local history, researched, talked about and written up by local people. It is very unusual to find people from Brighton doing field-work in Glasgow or Newtown, Powys. Local knowledge is the strongest card in the amateur's pack, but it is possible to be shamefully ignorant of the importance, or even the exist-ence, of something one passes every day. A few years ago a Wiltshire textile manufacturer with a keen interest in the history of the industry, was astonished to receive a telephone enquiry from the Science Museum about an old piece of spinning machinery in another factory just down the road from his own office. Although he was on the most friendly terms with the owners, he had no idea that they possessed such a splendid museum piece, regularly operated and in excellent condition.

This kind of situation is happening all the time, but the main cause of disaster – the demolition or scrapping of really

ALL GOODS AT LONDON STORE PRICES.

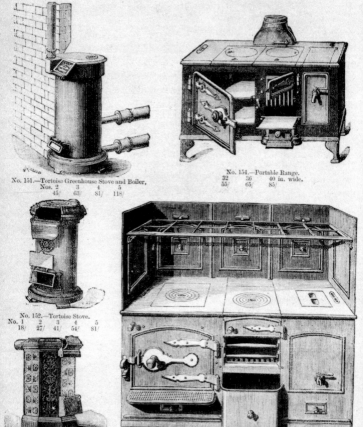

No. 151.—Tortoise Greenhouse Stove and Boiler,
Nos. 2   3   4   5
45/   63/   81/   118/

No. 154.—Portable Range.
32   36   40 in. wide.
55/   65/   85/

No. 152.—Tortoise Stove.
No. 1   2   3   4   5
18/   27/   41/   54/   81/

No. 153.—Tortoise Stove, with Tiles.
Nos. 1   2   3   4
38/9   59/3   84/   110/

No. 155.—Leamington Range.
With Oven and Large Side Boiler, Iron Covings and   4 ft. 6 in.   5 ft.
Plate Rack, bright mountings .. .. .. £9 10s. 0d. £10 10s. 0d.

**Experienced Workmen employed to fix Ranges and Fit up Hot Water Pipes to Bath Rooms, &c.
Estimates given and Efficiency guaranteed.**

The Articles illustrated in this Book represent but a small selection from those in Stock.

important historical evidence – is sheer ignorance and, paradoxically, the more recent the building or the equipment, the worse the ignorance is likely to be. Few people throw away an old suit or an old dress with any feeling that they may be robbing a costume museum of precious exhibits in the future and, in the same way, few manufacturers are likely to regard a twenty-year-old plastic-extruding machine or tile-press as of equal importance with a Watt steam engine. The old suit and the old extruding machine will be thrown away and replaced without a qualm of conscience, and in fifty years' time historians will be making frantic efforts to discover examples of them. What is obviously needed is a special kind of awareness and social responsibility that senses what is historically important before it becomes officially and fashionably historically important and, with the pioneering work now more or less safely accomplished, cultivating and spreading such an awareness is now probably the main task facing industrial archaeologists.

This change of emphasis is taking a little while to find general acceptance. There are still many enthusiasts who find it difficult to shake themselves free from the coal, iron and steam image with which industrial archaeology has grown up

A builders' merchant's catalogue, *c.* 1860.

Trade catalogues rarely have a long life. Like telephone directories, they are usually thrown away as soon as they become out-of-date. Some firms, however, have fortunately had the excellent habit of filing their old catalogues and advertising material and in a number of instances these files have subsequently found their way to public libraries and record offices. Other examples turn up from time to time in second-hand bookshops.

They are always to be treasured, partly for the sheer pleasure they provide and partly because, with their illustrations and their richness of detail, they help to make the history of business, of design and of manufacturing more real. Not infrequently, too, they document objects, such as pumps and concrete mixers, which were worked to death and of which no examples survive, either in or out of museums.

and who cannot yet see that the old Empire flying-boat slip-ways and hangars at Hythe and Broadcasting House, Portland Place, are just as interesting and important as the Iron Bridge and Box Tunnel. It would be something of an exaggeration to say that the Industrial Revolution of the eighteenth and nine-teenth centuries has been done to death, but industrial archaeo-logists cannot keep on treading the same ground for ever, especially when there is so much useful and urgent work to be done among the relics of the Second Industrial Revolution, the revolution based on electricity and petroleum. It is in this direction that the new generation of industrial archaeologists should be turning their eyes and devoting their energies, and this Pocket Book is intended to make it easier for them to do so.

Section One

The main tasks for industrial archaeology during the next ten years and the people to carry them out

Industrial archaeology is still a good name for the subject. It carries definite implications. There is, for instance, a difference between industrial history, which can be written entirely by using printed or manuscript sources, and industrial archaeology, which is based on systematic fieldwork, and on the organised study of physical remains. And the use of the word 'industrial' is neither casual nor vague. It binds the subject closely to that period of technological and economic development which is characterised by factories and employed labour, which means, in practical terms, to the eighteenth, nineteenth and twentieth centuries.

There are purists who would narrow down the time-range considerably, putting the emphasis firmly on evidence surviving from what is usually known as the Industrial Revolution, approximately 1750–1850. This seems unnecessarily restricting, because it ignores the very point of industrial archaeology – to provide facts about the history of industry and technology which are essential to balanced and comprehensive scholarship. What is available in libraries, archives and museums simply does not give the full picture, nor, in many instances, an accurate picture.

Industrial archaeology lessens the risk of historical errors. It adds an extra source of evidence to what can be extracted from books, business archives, letters, memoirs, prints and photographs. In order to build up a completely satisfying record, one must gather information from all the available fields. Industrial archaeology is no different from Roman or medieval archaeology in this respect. It complements the literary sources, so that the resulting facts and conclusions are more reliable than they would have been if we had been compelled to rely on either literature or archaeology alone.

It is unfortunately true that any historical evidence is

always inadequate. There is much, for instance, that we should like to know about the early days of the steam engine or of machine tools, or of plastics. We are frustrated in our search for information by the unfortunate fact that original equipment has been scrapped, drawings and other records thrown away, personal and business letters burnt. One cannot imagine any branch of industry or technology where the historian is not, to some extent, obliged to use his imagination and intuition in order to fill the gaps in the story.

Curiously enough, the difficulties do not grow less as we move closer to our own times. We should, by now, have become aware of the folly of getting rid of old plant or old records before calling in expert advice to discover if historically significant material is being threatened. But, in fact, matters have got worse, rather than better. This is mainly for

Brewery complex at Alton, Hampshire, c. 1965.
The buildings shown in this picture cover a period of getting on for two hundred years. The most modern, the Harp Lager brewery to the right, is not yet twenty years old and its owners would almost certainly take strong objection to its being described as industrial archaeology. Yet, as the photograph shows, there is no point in time at which industrial archaeology can be said to begin or end. The earliest and the most recent buildings on this site are here, not exactly for the beer, but for the exceptionally suitable and reliable water-supply. Few places can offer, on such a small area, as much archaeological evidence of the history of British brewing.

---

two reasons. Mergers, takeovers and shut-downs have become more frequent and the rate of technological advance has become more rapid. An old-established firm may be run by fully responsible people, anxious to safeguard their archives and proud of their traditions. It can, nevertheless, be bought out at any time – if it is a small family business, this is more likely to happen – and, almost before the old management has time to look round to see what is happening, control has passed to the new masters, the equipment is junked, the records, the board-room portraits and the furniture have all gone.

The fast-moving, fast-growing industries aim at getting the maximum use from new plant, amortising it as quickly as possible and replacing it with something more up-to-date, as soon as the accountants, the planners and the technical staff approve. The result is that, in many important instances, the recent growth of the industry is very poorly documented indeed. Nobody photographs or films the equipment in use in order to provide a record for the historians of the future to look at, nobody preserves detailed notes and statistics of the performance of machinery and equipment, nobody collects statements from the first people to use a new process, even though this may be of momentous importance. And nobody, certainly, preserves the earliest machine of what was a new type when it is eventually superannuated and replaced. What, for instance, has happened to the first tarmac-laying machine to appear in Britain, to the first pneumatic road-breaker, to

FIG. 220.

THE Concrete Mixer, Fig. 220, is engraved from a photograph of a form of Mixer that has been also extensively used by Engineers and Contractors, and was, we believe, first used in the construction of the Admiralty Pier at Dover, by Messrs. H. Lee & Sons; and it is generally known as Lee's Mixer. It consists of a wrought-iron cylinder placed diagonally on its axis, and is capable of taking a charge of one cubic yard of the materials to be mixed. This cylinder is fitted with charging doors at each end, which are made somewhat like a throttle-valve; the throat being bored out, and the revolving cover turned on its edge, it is opened by a toe-ended key from the outside, and when it closes it sweeps off from its seat any loose concrete hanging to it in a most effective manner; all other forms of doors having given trouble from the concrete accumulating and setting in the joints. Immediately the charge is let out at the bottom door and closed again, the upper one is opened, and the charge of dry materials, which have been measured into the hopper, is let in, and the top door closed, and the machine worked for about 12 to 20 revolutions, the stuff being thrown from end to end of the cylinder twice at each revolution. A water tank, with adjustable overflow, is always kept full by the lift and force pump shown, and a large valve and elbow pipe discharges the contents into the mixing vessel as each charge is put in.

The Machine is fitted with a Shoot, the point of which can be moved sideways sufficiently to discharge into either of the two drop bottom Skips (Fig. 214) which are placed in front of the Machine. The whole of the machinery is fitted in a wrought-iron framing of the form shown, and mounted on flanged travelling wheels to suit any gauge of rails, and the corners of the under frame are provided with blocking screws to render the Machine steady while at work, if on narrow gauge of rails; but on a wide gauge of rails these blocking screws are unnecessary.

A page from the catalogue, *c.* 1880, of Stothert and Pitt of Bath, the well-known manufacturers of civil engineering plant.

No concrete mixer of this period survives. This catalogue, which is itself a great rarity, together with advertisements in trade journals, is our only source of information about the mixer's construction, price and performance.

the first coal-cutter? Were pictures taken of them in use? Does any reliable information survive as to their performance and failure rates? It is extremely doubtful. Will British Rail eventually preserve the first of their mainline diesel locomotives to go into service, an event almost as epoch-making in its way as the early journeys of the Rocket?

The fact of the matter is that a great deal of modern industry – there are some most honourable exceptions – is so anxious to prove it is up-to-date, cost-conscious, growth-minded, forward-looking, that it finds itself faced with a serious psychological problem when a suggestion is made that it should pay a little attention to the past now and again. Eyes must be turned firmly and immovably to the front. History is treason.

One mentions all this only to indicate to the industrial archaeologist something of the climate within which he has to work and to provide clues to what the priorities in research and recording are likely to be.

Broadly speaking, anything in a rural area is likely to be less threatened than anything in a town or city. The reason for this is not that the local authorities in towns are less concerned with history or the national heritage. It is, unfortunately, a question of higher land values and greater pressure on space. The experience of the last thirty years, especially, has made it abundantly clear that even buildings of great and acknowledged importance have very little chance of survival if they are unfortunate enough to be on a site anywhere near the centre of a city or major town. Local authorities and Government departments turn a deaf ear, or produce some formula to the effect that the march of progress cannot be interrupted.

Railway and canal bridges and viaducts are practically certain to go, once they pass out of use. It is useless merely to get indignant about this. One must have a good deal of sympathy for the unfortunate owners. A bridge is an exceedingly expensive structure to maintain. The painting, inspection and repair work on a major bridge, especially an iron bridge, can very easily cost £10,000 or £20,000 a year. It is unreasonable to expect the transport undertaking itself to shoulder such a burden, and local and central government bodies are understandably unwilling to shift the cost onto the ratepayers and taxpayers. The only really satisfactory solution, whether the object to be preserved is a bridge, a mill, a pottery or anything else which has to be left on its original site if it is to be preserved at all, is to transfer the ownership to some form of trust mainly relying on private subscriptions and independent of changes in the political climate. This has already happened in one or two instances – the Conway Bridge is a notable example, the Abbeydale Forge, Sheffield, is another.

But even with the greatest imaginable amount of good fortune, very few industrial monuments are going to find Fate as kind to them as to Abbeydale or Conway. The number of old industrial buildings and machines which survive the determination of their owners to get rid of them will inevitably be remarkably small, and since this wish to demolish, scrap and remodel will be greatest among the more prosperous, dynamic concerns in the busiest places, the correct policy and strategy for industrial archaeologists is clear.

First priority for detailed recordings must be given to these categories of material:

1 Factory premises, commercial buildings and transport installations of all kinds in or near city centres.
2 Premises just taken over by another concern, especially if the firm bought out is an old-established firm of the family type.
3 Anything controlled by the British Railways Board or other nationalised industries under great financial pressure.
4 Machinery and plant layout, on any type of site belonging to a firm known to be in one of the more 'progressive' and more highly competitive industries.

To achieve adequate documentation or, indeed, any documentation at all in these cases, demands a first-class local intelligence system and very considerable powers of persuasion. One must discover what a firm possesses which can fairly be said to be of historical importance, one must have reasonable warning of any possibility of modernisation, shut-down or change of ownership, and one must somehow achieve a measure of co-operation from the firm concerned. This is why industrial archaeology depends so much on what might be called its troops on the spot, and why the range of these supporters and fieldworkers needs to be wide. It is the people on the staff of planning departments, of railways, of factories and industrial research departments, of builders and architects, of banks, of electricity, gas and water undertakings, who get to hear of impending changes and who are consequently such invaluable members of local industrial archaeology groups. It is the people who work in local factories, and run them, who are in a position to know what there is in them – material often totally unsuspected even by extremely well-informed national experts.

Very few concerns indeed are likely to shout from housetops that they possess a particularly ancient loom or steam engine or lathe. Their reticence is perfectly understandable. The equipment may be in excellent working order, but to confess its age may be felt to be commercially dangerous, bad for the image of the firm. If it has to be replaced, it may be safer to get rid of it quietly and say nothing.

Even if they do act in a responsible, public-spirited manner, and notify the local museum or industrial archaeology group that an item exists and that they are willing for it to be given a good home instead of breaking it up, they may discover that they have brought upon themselves problems of another order altogether, quite apart from losing the value of the scrap-metal, which may, in the case of large and heavy machinery, amount to several hundred pounds. Their new difficulty may be either that no museum is in a position to accept their proposed gift, or, should suitable storage or exhibition space exist, there are no funds available with which to pay for taking the machinery to pieces, and transporting it. This can be equally true of company records, especially engineering drawings, which, in the case of a very large organisation, such as the railways, can easily weigh hundreds of tons and need a large warehouse to accommodate them, in order that they can be given a preliminary sorting.

One or two large concerns – Guinness in Dublin is an outstanding example – have enlisted the help of an expert to go round their premises and draw up lists of equipment, large and small, which should be preserved if possible when the time comes to replace it. This is a new type of industrial consultant, and one hopes very much that such an excellent innovation will spread. Many, perhaps most, firms, however, are extremely suspicious of any outsider going round their works. They fear that closely guarded industrial secrets may reach their competitors, that eyes and ears admitted for one purpose may be used for another. There is little of any general value that can be said in answer to this, except that it is impossible to over-estimate the importance of the public relations side of industrial archaeology, and that this is one of those problems which, on occasions, can be solved only by making sure that one has friends inside the fortress, who will provide private information on interesting plant which is in danger of destruction. Developing such contacts, and making sure they are well-distributed among local industries, is an important preliminary to, if not an actual part of, research. It should certainly not be scorned.

If, of course, the friend at court can be the managing director or factory manager himself, so much the better. In the present writer's experience, the time spent in getting to know local management, and making sure that the aims and methods of industrial archaeology are appreciated, is immensely well spent. Industrialists are rarely difficult or obstructive unless they are forced to feel they are dealing with cranks, or unless the unreasonable is demanded of them, which comes to much the same thing. The unreasonable, in this context, can be defined as:

a Expecting the company to lose a substantial sum of money.

b Making promises which cannot be fulfilled, e.g. saying machinery or documents should go to a museum, instead of being destroyed, before checking that there is a museum willing and able to receive them.

c Exaggerating the importance of the material in question, so that what should be merely recorded is urged on the management as being worthy of preservation.

d Giving the impression that the company should rightly be in the museum business, as well as the manufacturing business. It is always pleasant to come across a company which does happen to run a private museum or a well-planned archives department, but one has absolutely no right to demand this, or even expect it.

All material which is in any way significant should be properly recorded, photographically and in other ways. This is a duty which companies and nationalised bodies should be educated to perform as a matter of routine, and in which local research groups should be willing and competent to give all possible assistance. Preservation is another matter altogether, and needs discrimination and common sense. Broadly speaking, one should attempt to support the preservation of any item only if one is quite sure that a superlative of some kind can be applied to it. It may, for instance, be the earliest surviving iron bridge, or the best-preserved woollen mill in the Cotswolds, or the only surviving colliery beam engine in Yorkshire still under steam, or the finest example of a needle

Passenger check-in at Heathrow Airport, 1946.

This particular photograph is preserved in the archives of the airline company known now as British Airways, but it could just as easily have been taken by someone who was about to make an air journey in those far-off and almost unbelievably primitive days.

No archaeological evidence of such a stage in aviation history can possibly remain. These tents were a temporary makeshift, put up or taken down in a few hours and tolerated only as long as something better could be provided. The only records are photographs and, even more important, the memories of the people who used and operated these primitive facilities. Collecting reminiscences of this kind is one of the industrial archaeologist's most useful and urgent activities. The photographs help him to ask the right questions.

mill still with the bulk of its original machinery, or the best of Rennie's bridges or Brunel's railway stations.

It is only industrial monuments of this exceptional quality which have any chance at all of being preserved in something approaching their original form. All the rest of the really important monuments will withstand destruction only if some other use can be found for them, a museum perhaps, a warehouse, another industry to occupy the old factory premises, conversion into a house or a youth hostel.

A great many interesting monuments are still with us today only because they have been more or less successfully adapted to a new purpose, in some cases to a succession of new purposes. A remarkably high proportion of the Gloucestershire and Wiltshire woollen mills of the eighteenth and nineteenth centuries, for example, have housed a variety of different industries since they made their last piece of cloth fifty or a hundred years ago. Their solid buildings have given a home to engineering, paint manufacture, milk-processing, rubber manufacture and the construction of pianos, to mention only a few random instances. In some cases the new industry has been established there so long that the industrial archaeologist may find it somewhat difficult to decide, when considering a particular building, if its main importance lies within the history of cloth-making or the history of rubber-making. The complete study of one industrial building, or group of buildings, can be a lengthy and complicated affair, demanding detailed investigation on the site, time-consuming discussions with elderly and retired workers, and a great deal of work in local archives and newspaper files.

The problem, in such a case, is to make a sensible distinction between short-term and long-term objectives. The short-term objective must be to decide if the building is sufficiently interesting and important to make a brief report on it, using, wherever possible, the standard record card issued by the National Survey of Industrial Monuments. This will almost certainly demand some work with printed sources, but it is wrong to defer filling in the card until one has exhausted all possible lines of enquiry with regard to the site. Such a stage can only be reached as part of a long-term objective, and it is quite possible for the short-term and the long-term work on a site to be carried out by different people. Suppose, for instance, that a large railway station is shortly to be demolished. The urgent task, obviously, is to make sure that as full a description as possible is carried out in the time available. This may necessitate a breakdown of labour, with perhaps six people taking photographs and making notes, in order that no detail shall be missed – the décor and furnishing of the waiting-rooms, the manufacture and dating of the lavatory equipment, the ticket-office, the telegraph and signalling installations, the refreshment room, the platform-construction, the lighting and so on. These records should go, typed and with photographs, to the local library. Five, ten, perhaps twenty years later, an historian may well consult them and embody them in a new standard work on railway architecture or in a biography of the man responsible for the original design. He will be profoundly grateful to his predecessors, working against the clock while the material was still there to be seen, for their care and their catholic interest in the site. No detail is too small to be remarked on, no part of the building lacking in potential significance.

Some of the most valuable work in industrial archaeology is being carried out by the people with an eye and a taste for small things. A fifteen-year-old schoolboy, known to the writer, began a survey, which eventually lasted more than two years, of all the man-hole covers and gutter-grids in his town of 20,000 people. Working meticulously with a street-plan of the town, he noted the maker's name on every casting, and the change of type from one area to another, and in this way he was able to make a very specialised and illuminating growth-map of the town, and, at the same time, to show how sources of supply changed from decade to decade. Other researchers have looked at bricks and lamp-posts, with a similar purpose in mind.

The long history of the rails used by the railways, public and private, is to be found written in the fences that have been made out of pensioned-off pieces of the permanent way. These were cut into suitable lengths and used as the uprights of the fence, sometimes to hold a wooden fence, sometimes one made very simply of gas-piping pushed through holes bored in the posts. A comparison of sections of these rails with the comprehensive collections of the British Transport Museum will often tell a story of an amalgamation, a shut-down, or a change of policy. Some of these long-lived fencing posts will be discovered to have travelled a very long way from the place where they were originally used for railway purposes.

By comparison with other branches of industrial archaeology, railways, windmills and canals have received more than their fair share of devotion. Other industries have been much less fortunate, and it may be useful to list some which are in pressing need of attention during the next few years.

1 Ports and harbours

What is wanted here is not the romantic, *Old Harbours of Cornwall*, type of book and article which has been appearing in fair profusion for half a century and more, but detailed descriptions of the layout, construction and present condition of the harbours, together with reliable information about any old equipment which survives, and about warehouses still standing.

2 Brick and tile works and potteries

These have been most inadequately treated so far. Large numbers of small works have gone out of production during the past thirty years. Most of them were in rural areas, or on the outskirts of towns, and are still there to be surveyed, although a number have been converted to other uses – particularly to the manufacture of breeze blocks and other concrete products.

3 Quarrying and gravel-working

It is a strange fact that no satisfactory book exists on either of these industries, although Britain has a most interesting range of areas, stone and methods of working. Satisfactory records of local quarries and stone mines are badly needed. Many have been filled in with coal waste and household and industrial refuse, and some, like the huge mines at Box and Corsham, near Bath, which are used by the Ministry of Defence as ammunition stores, are no longer free to be documented, at least by members of the public. But the great majority of British quarries which have been in operation at any time are still there to be seen, and many ancient quarrymen are still alive, with most useful historical and technical details to communicate to an investigator with a tape-recorder.

4 Factory chimneys

Here again, a most interesting book is waiting for an enthusiastic and knowledgeable author. Special local studies are also needed, to record details of design, materials and constructional techniques. Many factory chimneys are among the finest of our industrial monuments, and it is very desirable that some of the most beautiful brick and stone examples should be preserved, at a time when old chimneys are being felled at an increasing rate and when new ones are almost all of concrete, itself a most skilled technique. It may be noted in passing that a factory chimney is an essential part of the group of buildings to which it belongs and often gives much needed height and variety to the landscape. To urge the preservation of, say, a mill, and ignore the chimney that goes with it, is absurdly short-sighted.

5 Small country factories and workshops

The range of products one has in mind here is very wide. It includes, for instance, beer and cider, leather, boots and shoes, bacon, agricultural implements, ropes and nets, timber, lime and paper. With the growing centralisation of nearly all industries, a great many of the smaller units have been closed down in recent years, and their premises abandoned or converted to other uses. In a number of instances, however, a surprising amount of the old equipment remains, and it should be recorded quickly. There is an excellent opportunity, too, to collect information from people who once worked in these old concerns and who are very likely to have continued to live in the district.

6 Workhouses

These were a most important part of the national economy during the eighteenth and nineteenth centuries, but, for some reason, they have not, as buildings, received the attention they deserve. Most of them are still standing, and it is rare to come across one which has no architectural merit at all. Most of them, in fact, are fine buildings, well proportioned, well planned and well built, often on commanding sites, with large gardens. Their normal transformation has been into hospitals or old people's homes, and a good many changes have consequently been made in the internal arrangements. Even so, the shell and general plan of the buildings is usually much as it was, and a useful survey can be made. It is wise, before starting work, to consult the County or City Archivist and Librarian to see if the original plans and specifications survive, as they often

Stretching gloving-leather at C. and J. Pittard's works at Yeovil, Somerset, in 1935.

This is one of a set of photographs taken during a period of national economic depression, not to record industrial processes for posterity, but to serve as illustrations in a brochure designed to 'impress foreign buyers'. The firm no longer has a copy of the brochure itself and the preservation of the photographs is entirely fortuitous. They were 'put away in a drawer and forgotten', a common fate for historically valuable material of this kind. A thorough search would reveal similar items in a great many other offices and homes.

do, together, on occasion, with supporting information about the numbers to be accommodated.

7 Roads

All roads, apart from the motorways are, to a greater or lesser extent, an historical series of layers, and, as such, a remarkably interesting laboratory in which to study the way in which road-making techniques have changed, decade by decade. Roads are always having trenches opened up across them or along them, and most county or borough surveyors are willing to allow serious-minded people to examine a section of trench, provided they give some warning of their intentions and take care not to put themselves in any danger, and not to impede the progress of the work. One is looking particularly for the following evidence:

(a) *The composition of the original road*, the thickness of each layer, from foundation to surface, with the size and type of stone used, and any indication of whether it was packed, or merely dumped and spread.
(b) *Subsequent surfaces laid.*
(c) *Approximate date and thickness of the first tar macadam surface.*

The first item in (c) – the date – is usually difficult, if not impossible to decide, unless the information should happen to exist in the Surveyor's own departmental records, or in the archives to which these records have been transferred. The evidence in (a) is particularly interesting when the history of the original road is known, as for instance in the case of Telford's great road from London to Holyhead.

8 The aircraft industry

This covers both the manufacturing and the operating sides of military and commercial aviation. The industry in its early days was carried on at a considerable number of locations and even as late as the 1950s there were more than twenty factories in Britain producing aeroplanes. Most of these factories have now been converted to other uses and there is an urgent and important task to be carried out in accumulating the material, both written and oral, which will allow their history to be written.

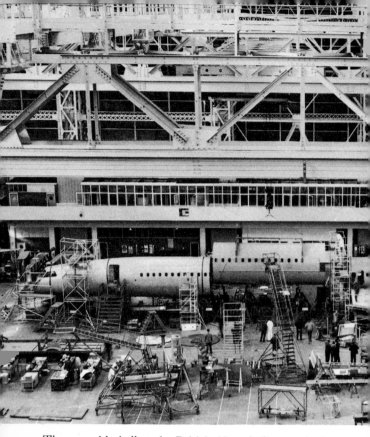

The assembly hall at the British Aircraft Corporation's factory, Filton, Bristol.

This is a company photograph, taken with the interests of BAC, not of industrial archaeologists, in mind. But, since outside photographers are rarely welcome in factories, one has to be content with what one can get and there is no doubt that historians fifty years from now will find a great deal to attract their attention in this picture. Beyond all doubt, everything it shows will appear incredibly antiquated by then, and it is most unlikely that either the British Aircraft Corporation or the assembly hall itself will have survived. Where, in that case, will the historian discover the photographs? In some suitable public archive, one hopes, but quite possibly among the family papers of some former employee of the company, who could not bear to see interesting pictures destroyed and took them home with him.

9 Oil, petrochemicals and synthetic fibres

Before 1939 the oil industry was on a very small scale. The major developments have taken place since 1945, with the building of refineries and petrochemical plants on a completely new scale. In the process the comparatively primitive, almost domestic, arrangements of the pre-war period have been largely forgotten and most of the evidence swept away. There is an important field of activity for industrial archaeologists here, in helping to recreate a picture of the industry as it was in the 1920s and 1930s.

10 Public utilities

The growth of the gas, electricity, water and telephone industries has been enormous during the past twenty-five years, and the installations of 1920 would seem primitive and parochial in the extreme, if they could be put back into service today. The small local power-stations, gas works, water-supply systems and telephone exchanges of that period have been made totally obsolete by the development of national grid systems and automatic installations. One cannot, for purely practical reasons, preserve a town gas works intact or transfer it to a museum, but there is much useful detective work and recording to be done in tracking down the bits and pieces which remain from the old days of these industries. Most of the gasholders, for instance, which still have a function for local storage, exist and some of them are very venerable indeed. It is interesting to study their design and their present condition, after so many years of useful service. In many towns, the former retort-house and office-building have not been pulled down, but converted to meet a wide range of entirely different purposes. So, too, have a number of the old electric power-stations, many of them dating back to the first decade of the present century.

These industries are given only as examples, and can be added to without difficulty. Rubber, shipbuilding, automobiles, machine-tools and agricultural implements are other important modern industries which come readily to mind. Whole categories of industries are waiting for a new generation of industrial archaeologists to tackle them and for a great deal of basic, on-the-spot work time is running out fast.

But the importance of industrial archaeology should not be absurdly exaggerated, as not infrequently happens, alas. It is an extremely valuable tool of scholarship, and another way of acquiring understanding of the past, but it is only one tool among many, and it has to be used in conjunction with a number of others in order to obtain reliable results. The person who is unaware of the guidelines provided by other branches of history – architectural, social, local, economic – is not likely to approach a mill or a turnpike house or a small harbour with his eyes very wide open.

The point of industrial archaeology being to provide evidence which is not otherwise available, it is very desirable to take certain preliminary steps to discover the extent of the facts which are already known. These will be of two kinds:

a General information about the history of a district, an industry or a craft;

b Specific details of particular sites.

But to say that facts are 'already known' is often misleading. They may exist, buried away in newspaper items of a century ago or in books long out of print. In such cases, the information one needs is quite possibly, for all practical purposes, unknown. It has to be rediscovered and reassessed in order to make it available once again, and for its present significance to be made clear.

A very good example of this is the mass of invaluable material contained in the advertisements published in local newspapers, from the eighteenth century onwards. Many of these concern the sale of property, and frequently provide the only reliable information we have about the ownership and name of the premises at a particular date, and about the work being carried on there. These advertisements are especially

Advertisement in the *Bath Chronicle*, 1809, for quarries to let.

Local newspapers are a most important source of information about industrial sites and processes. Combing through them demands a lot of time and an iron discipline – the temptation to let one's eyes stray over to fascinating, but irrelevant material of a different nature is hard to resist – but the effort can produce facts which are unobtainable in any other way.

useful where a building has changed its use, as often happened with industrial establishments. A Wiltshire mill, for instance, may have moved out of corn, into cloth and back again to corn, during a period of fifty years. If these fifty years were between 1790, say, and 1840, the sale announcements are likely to indicate a change in the source of power, water at the earliest dates and steam towards the end.

Local newspapers' files are surprisingly good, when one considers the conditions under which they have survived. Apart from the sets held nationally by the British Museum, in its newspaper and periodical collection at Colindale, most local libraries have long runs of newspapers published in their area. Quite often, these go back to the earliest days of the paper. In some cases, files are also to be found and consulted at the office of the newspaper itself.

It has to be admitted, nevertheless, that ploughing through newspaper files in search of information, however precious, is a tedious and time-consuming affair. On the other hand, it is undoubtedly a pursuit with attractions of its own, and there are few better ways of getting the feel of a period than by browsing through ten years of the local paper. One may often come across items which lead one along paths very different

Lot 3. All that FREEHOLD MESSUAGE or DWELL-ING-HOUSE, with a large Piece of Ground adjoining, containing in front, next the turnpike-road leading from Bradford to Briſtol, 40 feet, and extending in depth backwards of the ſame breadth 200 feet, or thereabouts, ſituate at a place called Croſs-Way Place, on Coombe-Down, in the ſaid pariſh of Widcombe; now and for ſome time paſt in the poſſeſſion of the ſaid John Sersce, the bankrupt.

The Ground attached to this lot is pleaſantly ſituated, and well adapted for building on, and there is no ground rent, or other outgoing, payable thereont.

Lot 4. All that FREESTONE QUARRY, containing one acre or thereabouts, ſituate on Coombe-Down aforeſaid, now and for ſome time paſt alſo in the poſſeſſion of the ſaid John Scrace; and held for the remainder of a term of 500 years, at the yearly rent of 1s. for the firſt 30 years, and 20s. yearly during the reſidue of the term.

To this lot will be attached a ſhare or uſe in a Crane and two Windlaſſes; and theſe two laſt lots will alſo be ſold ſubject to ſuch ſum of money as is charged thereon by way of mortgage.

For view of the ſeveral premiſes apply to Mr. R. Harris, No. 14, Walcot-ſtreet, Bath; and for particulars and conditions of ſale, to Meſſrs. Leman, ſolicitors, Briſtol.
(One Concern.)

from those indicated in the original plan of research, but the result can easily be a considerably improved perspective and understanding.

It is, in any case, possible to exaggerate the time needed to work through twenty or thirty years of a weekly paper. The task is not as terrifying as it may seem. Once the layout of the paper becomes familiar, one can skim through an issue surprisingly quickly, in search of relevant material. Having found something of interest, the best plan is usually to copy it out if it is brief, and to get the library to provide a photocopy if it is of any length. This service is cheap and saves a great deal of one's personal time.

Browsing-material is not, of course, confined to newspaper files. The pamphlet boxes of most libraries are an important source of facts for the student of industrial history. Two types of pamphlet are worth looking for, those issued by estate agents to give details of a property which is about to be sold, and those which celebrate some special occasion in the history of a firm – an Open Day, perhaps, or the opening of a new works, or an amalgamation. Quite a lot of this kind of publicity material – pamphlets, leaflets and posters – survives in the offices of estate agents themselves, and it is always worth consulting an old-established concern to see what they may have, with the warning that where material has been preserved in any quantity it is almost certain to be stored in no meaningful order and to be exceedingly dusty. Items of interest to the industrial archaeologist will always be in a very small minority, except in the case of one or two specialist, and usually London-based firms, dealing in plant and machinery. Whether in a library or museum or in the cellars and attics of private offices, the bulk of these old publications will inevitably concern houses, especially large houses, farms and estates, and even here survival is extremely chancy. One needs plenty of time and patience.

The main problem, of course, is to be able to see the wood for the trees in order to discover three things:

a Whether the particular piece of research is worth doing at all.

b How it fits into the larger pattern of what is known about the industry.

c The most economic method of getting at the information which will make proper sense of one's fieldwork, and lead to a more satisfactory final report.

The short answer is to take good advice in the first place. This will normally mean attaching oneself to a local research group (see the list of groups in Section Five of this book) where priorities are discussed and where a pooling of experience is taking place continuously, among people with a wide range of interests. The group will, in most cases, have close links with university lecturers and other experts, who can be very helpful in suggesting worthwhile research projects and, conversely, in preventing the enthusiastic amateur from wasting his time on matters of small significance, and from labouring in fields which have already been adequately tilled by other people.

The fact remains, however, that in industrial archaeology as in everything else, there is no short cut to knowledge. The more information one has absorbed, and the better disciplined and organised it is, the more satisfactory each piece of further research and recording is likely to be.

Everybody, however, wherever he lives and works, can read one short book which will help him greatly to understand what is worth doing, and why. It is Professor W. H. Hoskins' *Local History of England* (1959). Industrial archaeology is, first and foremost, a form of local history, and the great value of Professor Hoskins' book is that it shows how this specialised branch fits in with all the other branches. It stresses throughout what is often forgotten, that history is primarily about people. 'One can all too easily', he says, 'criticise the average local historian for his remorseless and undiscriminating collection of details; but it is detail, rightly selected, that finally illuminates the generalisations, all the talk about taxable wealth and social classes, wage-levels, and price movements. One must never forget that history is about people; and the local historian least of all should need this reminder.' (p. 105.)

A large literature of industrial archaeology has appeared during the past twenty years. The most comprehensive and up-to-date book list can be found in Neil Cossons' *The B.P. Book of Industrial Archaeology* (1975), which is itself an excellent guide to the history of the main technical developments of the past two hundred years and to a large number of the principal sites. R. A. Buchanan's Pelican, *Industrial Archaeology in Britain* (1972), follows a similarly machines-and-buildings oriented approach. In my own recent paperback, *Exploring Our Industrial Past* (1975), I have put a stronger emphasis on the workers who used the machines, and this philosophy, which is developed at greater length in the new edition of my *Industrial Archaeology: a New Introduction* (1976), might be summarised as industrial archaeology-with-people.

The basic practical techniques required for fieldwork are described in J. P. M. Pannell's book, *The Techniques of Industrial Archaeology*, which was originally published in 1966 and has since (1973) appeared in a revised form, edited by J. Kenneth Major.

Photographic inspiration of a high order is provided by Eric de Maré, for black and white photography, in *The Functional Tradition in Early Industrial Building* (1958: reprinted 1968), and, for colour, Brian Bracegirdle's pictures in *The Archaeology of the Industrial Revolution* (1973) are unsurpassed and probably unsurpassable.

Section Two

Industrial archaeology and the law

In Britain, as elsewhere, the law concerns industrial archaeologists in two ways. It affects both the material in which they
are interested and their own rights as citizens and researchers.

The first industrial archaeologists to find themselves in
difficulties with the law to any considerable extent were railway
enthusiasts, or rather that special brand of railway enthusiast
whose principal activity and pleasure consists of engine-
spotting. Some engine-spotters are also engine-photographers,
but for the most part the whole point of this rather curious
exercise is to note the number of a locomotive and to check it
off against a classified list.

In itself, this is a perfectly legal and harmless activity, and
many a boy has progressed from engine-spotting to a wider and
more profound interest in railway matters and, indeed, to
industrial archaeology in general. Clashes with authority are
likely to occur only when the engine-spotter, in his eagerness
to increase his productivity, takes up his position in places
where British Rail or the police would prefer him not to be.
The regulations on this point do not appear to be well understood and a little explanation may be helpful.

Nobody, engine-spotter or not, is permitted to be where the
railway by-laws say he may not be. Such forbidden places
include embankments, grass verges inside the railway fence,
sidings, yards, engine-houses and any part of the track. Anyone
found on such territory without the permission of a competent
railway official is liable to prosecution. The fact that one may
happen to be an archaeologist or an engine-spotter gives one
absolutely no privilege or exemption, however desirable or
suitable the forbidden spot may be.

Railway stations are another matter, and it is here that the
main problem is likely to be found, sometimes in an unpleasant form. Anyone may legitimately pass a barrier and
enter a platform, provided he is equipped with a valid train
ticket or platform ticket. What he may not do, ticket or no

ticket, is to make a nuisance of himself to other passengers or to interfere in any way with the operation of the railway. If he does either of these things, railway officials are entitled to remove him, with or without the help of the police, and, if necessary, arrest him and bring him to court. In this respect, the engine-spotter may find himself in exactly the same legal position as a drunk or a prostitute or a member of the IRA with bombs in his pocket. The law does not want him to be where he is and will take the steps required to move him elsewhere. In practice, British Rail is normally indulgent and friendly towards engine-spotters, except where they are present in such numbers as to inconvenience other members of the public or to make it difficult for railwaymen to carry out their work. On some stations, such as Reading, those who are there solely for the purpose of noting engine-numbers are required to stand at a particular end of the platforms and notices are clearly posted to this effect. It should be emphasised, perhaps, that there have been extremely few prosecutions of engine-spotters. The railways, like any other organisation, depend a good deal on satisfactory relations with the public and taking people to court is not calculated to improve these relations. In any case, the great majority of engine-spotters are perfectly law-abiding and well-behaved.

But during the past ten years the whole country, not merely British Rail, has become much more security conscious and consequently much more inclined to tell members of the public where they can and cannot go. This change of attitude has several causes – IRA attacks, the increase in organised crime, the demands of insurance companies and the growth of a large and powerful security industry, which has a vested interest in keeping strangers away from the premises it receives large sums of money to guard.

As a consequence, industrial archaeology has become a more difficult business. Nowadays, caretakers, security officers and the police are much more suspicious of strangers with cameras and notebooks than they used to be, and many previously accessible sites, such as the West India docks, can no longer be visited. No permission is needed to photograph the exterior of a building, provided the picture is taken from the public highway and provided the subject of the photograph is not controlled by the Official Secrets Act. There is also no legal barrier to taking photographs through a window or to obtaining information either by the naked eye or with binoculars in the same way, so long as one remains entirely on the highway. The situation is, however, complicated by the fact that photography may be, and frequently is, banned in places which are regularly used by the public. These can include museums, shops and department stores, airport buildings, theatres, hotels and restaurants.

The law relating to trespass needs careful attention. Trespass arises whenever one person enters unlawfully upon land or a building which is in the possession of another person. There are several popular fallacies about this and two important points should be noted. The first is that trespass is not a crime, unless there is an Act of Parliament which makes the trespass a criminal offence. Under certain statutes it is, for example, a criminal offence for an unauthorised person to cross a railway line or to enter a Government airfield. Secondly, it is not necessary, to constitute a trespass, that actual damage should be done to the land or building on which the trespasser has set foot. The essence of the tort relating to trespass is interference with the possession of the other party, and this may arise by merely walking across his field, or throwing refuse on it, or placing or erecting anything on the land, even temporarily, without the other party's consent. Any act of physical interference is sufficient, and physical interference can amount to nothing more than one's unwanted presence.

The golden rule is therefore not to attempt to enter private property without having obtained permission previously. The law of trespass does not, however, relate to a public footpath which runs through private property, nor to photography from the air. One does not control or own the airspace, at any altitude, above one's property, unless the Official Secrets Act is involved, and no permission is required to reproduce or use aerial photographs. It is equally legal to obtain photographs or information from a vantage point in or on another building, from a hill or bridge, or from the top of a vehicle on the public highway.

The preservation of historic buildings, industrial or otherwise, is the concern of the Department of the Environment and of the Secretary of State for Wales and for Scotland, whose powers are derived from five Acts of Parliament: the Historic Buildings and Ancient Monuments Act, 1953; the Town and Country Planning Act, 1962; the Local Authorities (Historic Buildings) Act, 1962; the Civic Amenities Act, 1967; and the Town and Country Planning Act, 1968. Under these Acts, which have been supplemented in certain details by the Town and Country Planning Act, 1971, the authorities concerned have been required to compile lists of buildings which are considered to be of special historic or architectural interest. It is important to notice that the Minister may take into account, not only the building itself, but 'the desirability of preserving, on the ground of its architectural or historic interest, any feature of the building consisting of a man-made object or structure fixed to the building or forming part of the land and comprised within the curbilage of the building'. This very important provision means, in plain terms, that it is possible to schedule for preservation not only the building or site itself, but machinery and equipment associated with it.

Broadly speaking, the older the building, the better its chance of preservation and survival, which is by no means a satisfactory policy. In practice, this has meant the listing of everything built before 1700 which is in anything like its original condition; most buildings of 1700 to 1840; and a fairly ruthless selection of buildings after 1840. In drawing up the lists, four criteria have been kept particularly in mind:

a The value of the building as an illustration of a type or of social and economic history. Buildings of this kind would include railway stations, town halls, mills, prisons, theatres and workhouses.

b Technological importance, as in the case of early cast-iron structures, pre-fabrication or pioneering bridges and factories made of reinforced concrete.

c Links with famous events or characters.

d Value as an item or items in a group, such as terraces, squares or model villages.

The listing is carried out in two stages. After the Department's inspectors have carried out a survey, a provisional list is drawn up for each local authority area. This classifies buildings in three grades. Grade 1 contains buildings which are considered to be of outstanding interest – about 4% of the total; Grade 2, 'buildings of special interest, which warrant every effort to preserve them'; and Grade 3, buildings which are 'important enough to be drawn to the attention of local authorities and others, so that the case for preserving them can be fully considered'. Opinions and fashions change, however, and during the past ten years many buildings which were originally Grade 3 have been promoted to Grade 2, particularly when they possess what is known to the planners as 'group value'.

'Group value' is particularly likely to arise in the case of 'conservation areas', which were a creation of the Civic Amenities Act of 1967. 'Every local planning authority', says the Act, 'shall from time to time determine which parts of their area, or in Scotland district, are areas of special architectural or historic interest the character of which it is desirable to enhance, and shall designate such areas (hereafter referred to as "Conservation Areas" for the purpose of this section).'

The statutory lists are based on the provisional lists, but are not identical with them, since a good deal of argument may occur in relation to particular items. One can inspect the statutory lists during normal office hours on Mondays to Fridays, at Council offices; at the National Monuments Record, Fielden House, Great College Street, London SW1; at the Welsh Office, in Cardiff; and at the Scottish Office, in Edinburgh. At some Council offices, a certain amount of persistence and firmness may be necessary before the list is produced.

The statutory lists do not, for some unexplained reason, contain the gradings shown in the provisional lists, but the provisional lists, too, are open for inspection once the corresponding statutory lists have been issued. A study of either kind of list will show that the proportion of industrial buildings is still very small, although there has been a significant increase since the late 1960s.

Listing does not mean that a building has to be preserved intact under all circumstances, nor that funds will be available to carry out any conservation work which may be necessary. In this last respect, Britain lags behind several continental countries. France, for example, obliges the owner of a scheduled building to maintain it in a satisfactory condition. If he fails to do so, the work may be carried out by the State and the cost recouped from the owner. What the British legislation does lay down, however, is that demolition of a listed building is not permitted until the case for it has been fully examined and that any alterations must, so far as possible, preserve the character of the building. To do either of these things requires 'listed building consent', for which application has to be made to the local planning authority. If an owner proceeds without listed building consent, the penalty can be a fine of unlimited amount or up to twelve months' imprisonment, or both.

There have, unfortunately, been a number of occasions on which owners have decided to take the law into their own hands, or to make the provisions difficult to enforce. The three most common ways of achieving this are to fail to carry out even the minimum amount of maintenance and to allow a building to deteriorate for so long that it passes the point at which restoration is possible. At that stage, it is difficult for a local planning authority to object to demolition. Another much-favoured and deplorable method of ridding oneself of a listed encumbrance is to set fire to the building, and yet another is to demolish first, and then to deal with any trouble afterwards. The usual defence on such occasions is either ignorance of the fact that the building is listed or the unauthorised and irresponsible behaviour of an employee or sub-contractor. In theory, none of these things can happen and since 1967 there have been legal provisions to prevent and discourage it. Under the Planning Act, 1968, and the Civic Amenities Act, 1967, anyone who 'does or permits the doing of any act which causes or is likely to result in damage' to a listed building is liable on summary conviction to a fine not exceeding one hundred pounds. Such a small fine is no deterrent whatever to someone who sees the possibility of making many thousands once the old building is out of the way.

Whatever the law may say, an unscrupulous owner does not, in practice, find himself faced with too much of a problem, and some further form of control seems inevitable, probably along French lines. In theory, anyone who breaks the law by destroying a listed building in order to make some other use of the site, can be disciplined by having planning permission for a new building refused, but it takes a very tough local Planning Officer to carry out such a policy and the most that happens is usually considerable delay.

In certain circumstances, grants and loans are available to the owners of listed buildings, but listing does not automatically entitle one to financial help of this kind. The Department itself has powers to make grants only for the repair or maintenance of buildings which are of outstanding architectural or historic importance, that is, for buildings classified as Grade I on the provisional lists. Local authorities have greater discretion. They are allowed to make grants or loans for any building which they consider to be of architectural or historic interest and their choice is not restricted to outstanding or even to listed buildings. A condition of such a grant may be that there shall be an agreement 'for the purpose of enabling the public to have access to the property or part thereof during such period and at such times as the agreement may provide'.

Where it appears to the Minister that reasonable steps are not being taken for properly preserving a listed building, he may, if he thinks fit, authorise a local council to acquire it by compulsory purchase, together with 'any land comprising or contiguous to it which appears to the Minister to be required for preserving the building or its amenities, or for affording access to it, or for its proper control or management'.

It not infrequently happens that, on the basis of new information, a building is seen to be more important, sometimes much more important, than had been at first supposed, and to deserve listing. Listing is, however, a lengthy process and, where it appears to the local planning authority that an unlisted building is a special architectural or historic feature of the area 'and is in danger of demolition or of alteration in such a way as to affect its character as such', the owner and occupier of the building may be served immediately with a 'building preservation notice'. This comes into force immediately and lasts for six months, during which time the Minister has to make up his mind as to whether the building should be added to the list.

An actual instance will show how the building preservation notice and listing procedures work, and how a local industrial archaeology society can usefully apply pressure on the various bodies concerned.

At Downton, near Salisbury, a paper-mill began production in the 1740s. The buildings were considerably modified and expanded during the early nineteenth century and in the 1880s the mill was taken over by Wiggins, Teape, whose successor, Mark Palmer and Son, continued to make paper there until the early 1920s. The buildings were then converted to produce electric power, using a water-turbine, first for the adjacent tannery and then for the village. The power-station eventually passed into the ownership of the Central Electricity Generating Board, and was finally closed in 1971. The turbine was made by the well-known Hampshire engineering firm, Armfield's of Ringwood.

The buildings, which had been used for grinding corn before they were adapted to paper-making, are in a pleasant rural setting and of considerable charm. After ceasing to be used as a power-station, they were bought by a local builder, who proposed to use them for housing. At that point, the South Wiltshire Industrial Archaeology Society got wind of the scheme and applied, under the provisions of the 1968 Act, for a building preservation notice and for listing.

The first reply from the Department of the Environment said that there was no investigator of historic buildings available at that time to inspect the building. 'If however you have clear, up-to-date photographs of the building which you could lend us,' the letter went on, 'it may be possible to assess listability without a visit being made. It would also be helpful if you could let us have a sketch-plan showing the position of the building in relation to the surroundings.'

The Society sent the material required, supported by three reasons why it felt listing was justified. As they said, these were:

1 The building represents three stages of adaptive use – corn, paper, electricity – and is an excellent example of how these solidly-built little mills moved from one niche to another in the local economy. It has been much used by teachers in Wiltshire schools and colleges to illustrate this point and its educational value is considerable.
2 In its power-station days it was an early example of the usefulness of water-turbines in rural areas.
3 The site as it stands now has very marked amenity value, and this could be improved by careful treatment and planning.

This letter to the Department of the Environment was supplemented by another to the local Member of Parliament, setting out the facts and asking for his help.

From that point onwards, the Department moved with exemplary speed, although with some misunderstanding of what the Salisbury Society had been asking for. A few months earlier, they had, it appeared, been in touch with the Central Electricity Generating Board about the possibility of scheduling Downton Power Station as an industrial monument, but they had eventually decided 'not to press any longer for its retention'. This, they said, 'was because we had been assured by the Science Museum that a similar example of the same kind of engine (*sic*) from the Ringwood Power Station in Hampshire had already been earmarked as a museum exhibit'. They felt they could not press the Board to preserve both, 'and as the Hampshire one was of earlier date we settled for

Ringwood. We are waiting for the Science Museum to confirm that the Ringwood turbine is safely in store. According to our advisers, there are others of this type and that at Downton is not unique.'

However, 'having taken appropriate professional advice', the Secretary of State was satisfied that 'the building itself is of special architectural or historic interest' and he was therefore 'arranging for it to be added to the statutory list very shortly'.

The Downton turbine and generating equipment was thought by the Department to be 'worth preserving if a Museum could be found to take custody of it'. Together with the Ringwood engine, it was 'one of some 2,500 pieces of technological material which the Electricity Council on the advice of the Science Museum have identified for museum conservation and preservation'.

The Salisbury Society accepted the situation, realising that half a loaf was better than nothing at all. It wrote to the CEGB, mentioning that the plant would have to be stored until some suitable place could be found for it to be exhibited, and adding that 'a degree of specialist knowledge will be necessary in the re-siting and reconnection of the various mechanical and electrical components and circuitry'. Could the Board advise 'whether installation and wiring diagrams exist and by what means they can be made available and also if the necessary engineering expertise could be made available by the CEGB in the interests of completing the job satisfactorily'.

The situation outlined above could be described as 'above average'. There was an active local society – in fact, two; the South Wiltshire Industrial Archaeology Society and the Downton Society – a quick-acting and sympathetic Member of Parliament, co-operative and public-spirited owners and a Government department which responded rapidly once it was prodded in the right places and by people who knew what they were doing. The whole episode makes clear that the skills required by the industrial archaeologist are quite as much political and legal as they are technical.

Nevertheless, the Downton episode contains a number of unsatisfactory features, all of which have unfortunately been repeated many times elsewhere. The first is that, within the Department of the Environment, the left hand did not know what the right was doing. At one moment the South Wiltshire Society was told that no investigator was available to inspect the site and give an opinion on it, and, at another, that consultation with the Science Museum and other experts had already been going on for several months. The second regrettable aspect of the affair is that even in 1974, after industrial archaeologists had been doing their best to educate Government departments and local authorities for many years, it was still possible and indeed normal for those in positions of power to see an industrial building and the plant within it as two entirely separate things, meriting different treatment. It was proper for the building to be listed and looked after where it stood and for the machinery to be removed to a store and then, hopefully, to a museum.

This is an excellent instance of how the law can be observed in the letter, but not in the spirit. The fact that the Ringwood turbine is earlier and possibly finer, from an engineering point of view, than the Downton turbine, is irrelevant and reflects a sadly old-fashioned, pre-environmental attitude. The Science Museum collects turbines and steam engines as other people collect butterflies and birds' eggs. Its staff instinctively see a piece of machinery as a potential addition to their collection, to be accepted if it fills a gap and rejected if it is a duplicate or a less worthy example of something they already have. It is concerned solely and entirely with documenting an abstract, scholarly and largely sterile concept known as the history of technology.

The industrial archaeologist's attitude is quite different. To him, the object in its original setting is much more meaningful than the object transferred to a museum, however good that museum may be in its own right. Seen working and making electricity for the local community, an engine has a complete story to tell. The turbine and generating equipment installed in its little red-brick mill-building by the side of a pleasant Wiltshire river makes social, architectural, aesthetic and technical sense. An empty building in one place and a set of machinery in another do not add up to the same thing at all, no matter how much money and skill may be devoted to conserving, presenting and 'interpreting' them. Who gains if a bus-load of schoolchildren has to be taken to Downton to view the building and to the Science Museum or any other museum to see the turbine, dynamo and switchgear? The answer is 'nobody but the collector of technical butterflies'.

In this, as in other cases, the Secretary of State was not well advised and the local industrial archaeology societies clearly have many years' hard campaigning ahead of them before the position can really be said to have improved to any significant extent. And, to help the campaign along, it is invaluable for every society to have one or two lawyers, planners and people taking part in local politics among their more active members.

It might be usefully pointed out, with no wish to suggest that industrial archaeology is any more dangerous a pursuit than cricket or birds'-nesting, that any society with its wits about it will make it clear to its members in writing that it will not be held legally responsible for any accident or injury which may happen during an outing or excursion and that members take part in these events entirely at their own risk, exactly as if they were on their way to the paper shop or the bus stop. However, those who run museums and site exhibitions and invite the public to visit them have a legal obligation to render such places reasonably safe and they may well be successfully sued if it can be shown that they have failed to do so.

If a society or museum should happen to employ and pay people to carry out work, a different set of considerations comes into force. Such people are the servants of the society and they are entitled to bring an action for damages, which they will win if they can prove negligence.

A society is not liable, as a society, for any illegal act performed by one of its members during any activity carried out by the society. A member may steal a café tea-pot during a break for refreshment, make off with half a steam engine, or wreck a mill-wheel in a fit of maniacal frenzy. In such cases, which are uncommon, the individual responsible may have proceedings brought against him, but the society itself has committed no offence, however much moral responsibility it may feel.

Section Three

Processing and presenting one's finds

Nobody need feel under any more compulsion to communicate industrial archaeology discoveries than to communicate the experience of a sunset or a smile or a garden. It is still perfectly legal and respectable to do things for one's own pleasure and enlightenment.

But, assuming that one does have an urge to share one's knowledge with other people, there are certain useful and satisfying ways of setting about it – bearing in mind that, however limited one's ambitions, if something is worth doing at all, it is worth doing well. There is no more pleasure to be gained from playing industrial archaeology badly than from playing tennis badly. The difficulty is, unfortunately, that one knows all too well when one's tennis is bad, but it is all too easy to be deceived about the standard of one's industrial archaeology.

No harm can be done, therefore, by setting out a simple order of procedure, divided into three parts – observation, recording, communication.

Observation

It is a truism to say that one sees what one expects to see, which is another way of saying that one sees what it is fashionable and respectable to see. Since fashions and notions of respectability are constantly changing, this means, inevitably, that different generations notice and mention different things. Education, sex and social background all condition our powers of observation. Placed in front of the same object at the same time, no two people in a group of ten or fifty or a hundred will respond to it precisely alike. The variations may be very considerable indeed.

For this reason, a really complete and competent piece of recording cannot be carried out by one person, however experienced, intelligent and well-informed he or she may be.

Industrial archaeologists get much better results when they hunt in pairs, especially mixed-interest pairs. Two engineers, two architects or two economic historians make a deadening combination. Each person needs to feel that his eyes are different from those of his companion.

But, whether or not this very desirable variety can be achieved, certain principles of observation can be recommended:

1 Forget about what one believes one ought to notice. Concentrate on what one finds interesting and significant. If the bricks seem unusually large, or the doorway unusually low or narrow, or a room very hot or very cold, write that fact down.

2 Always try to imagine what it was like to work in the place one is visiting, what the noise level was, how it all smelt and what the pleasant and the unpleasant things about the job may have been. Think of yourself doing it and about going home at the end of a day's work.

3 Ask simple, basic questions about the organisation of the job and the working day – what time did the workers start and finish; how long did they have for their lunch and where were they expected to eat it; where did they put their outdoor clothes; how was the workshop heated, if at all; what was the discipline like; where were the lavatories and wash-places, if any; what kind of skill was required and how was it learnt.

4 Only after making a big effort along these lines, to get the historical feeling of the building, turn to the details of the machinery and other technicalities.

5 If the purpose of something or the method of operation isn't clear, ask someone else what it was for and how it worked. If you happen to be on your own, make a note of the problem and get an answer as soon as you can. Don't pretend to understand if you haven't.

Recording

Divide your notes into two sections – factual material and impressions. Remember that both are equally valid and that any conversation you may be lucky to have with former workers will and should provide you with both facts and feelings. Don't fall into the trap of believing that the facts are more important than the feelings. Both, in their different ways, are equally significant and valuable.

As a discipline and a spur to further curiosity and effort, ask yourself two questions:

1 'Am I putting down on paper or showing in a photograph everything that people a hundred years from now are likely to want to know about this place?'
2 'What information would I like to have about this, if it had disappeared fifty or a hundred years ago?'

Communication

Try to build up a picture of the kind of people you have to communicate with. What use are they likely to make of what you are putting into words or pictures? Your customers may be:

1 Fellow-enthusiasts for watermills, pumps, coal-mines or canal locks
2 People writing books and on the watch for new material
3 Historians of one kind or another, checking up on theories
4 Local journalists in search of something new

and many other types, including, as always, academics in search of thesis-fodder.

Ask yourself at what level the information is likely to be required. What you have and what you decide to give are certain to be very different. The quantity of information you put across should be much less in a talk than in an article, where everything can be re-read and pondered over. A talk or a lecture ought to be at least mildly inspirational, whereas something less warm may be appropriate in a piece of written communication.

One's store of knowledge can, of course, be given to the outside world in different measure on different occasions. The simplest and briefest form of communication consists merely of locating the site, in such terms as:

| Menai suspension bridge | Map no. 107 | Grid reference SH 556714 |

or

| Abbey Mills sewage pumping station, West Ham | Map no. 161 | Grid reference TQ 388832 |

A basic recording, of the type required by the National Survey of Industrial Monuments and entered on one of the Survey's standard record cards, would provide the following information, concerning a range of derelict colliery workshops (1839–41) at Haigh, near Wigan.

Description: dimensions; present condition; architectural features, etc.

HAIGH SAWMILLS   Prior to 1865, when the Wigan Coal and Iron Co. was formed, these were the central workshops for Lord Balcarres' extensive Haigh and Aspull Collieries. After the formation of Wigan Coal and Iron Co. they were used mainly as sawmills for the collieries and the large iron and steel works at Kirkless and for the repair of the Co.'s canal barges.

A fine range of stone buildings of architectural merit with central block and bell turret.

In ruinous condition.

Machinery and Fittings   Nothing left. Previously circular and pit saws, forge, blacksmith's fires, lathes, etc. driven by steam engines.

Danger of Demolition or Damage   Demolition already arranged for.

Printed, Manuscript or Photographic Records   NCB and Haigh Estate may have manuscript records. Photographs on back of card and others in possession of reporter.

This card is somewhat above the average of those filed by the National Survey. It gives the essential facts about the buildings and their history, makes a brief assessment of their value before demolition takes place, and offers one or two clues to anyone who wishes to follow the story up in greater detail.

It is only a small step from a record card entry of this quality to the kind of description which meets the requirements of the economic historian. Here is an example from Jennifer Tann's *Gloucestershire Woollen Mills* (1967, p.231). It is written by an academic with a considerable reputation in the field of industrial archaeology.

This extract relates to Dunkirk Mills, Nailsworth.

'When they replied to the factory inspector's enquiries concerning the date of their mill, Playne and Smith said that "part was very old; part built 1800, 1818, 1819, 1820 and 1821, we believe it has been a fulling mill more than 200 years".

Some of the surviving buildings date from the late 18th century but nothing is known of the site before this. In 1814 John Cooper was making cloth at the mill, but by 1820 Peter Playne was in occupation. By 1830 the firm was known as Playne and Smith. There was both water and steam power at the mills in the early 1830s, the water power varying from 40 h.p. to 10 h.p. In 1838 power looms were installed in the mills and in 1840 there were two in addition to the 71 hand looms (four of which were not in use). At this date, the mills were the most valuable of any in the Nailsworth valley except Longfords, the annual rental being £405. In 1844 the firm was known as Peter and Charles Playne, and in the 1860s and 1870s as P. C. and P. F. Playne. The mill ceased cloth production in c. 1890. In 1891 W. Walker and Sons, who had a large hosiery factory in Nottingham, bought Dunkirk Mills. They "left nothing but the shell of the building, entirely remodelling the interior to adapt it to their purpose. Among other improvements was the substitution of a modern steam engine in place of the old beam engine . . . the engine can instantly be coupled with the water wheel or the water wheel with the dynamo.

It was reputed to have the best water power in the Nailsworth valley and until 1940 four water wheels were in working order. A long high leat took water to the wheels, which were situated in pairs at right angles to one another. The stone mill is four storeys high and consists of one main range with small wings at either end." '

The sources of this information are given – ten local directories, Parliamentary Papers, and *Industrial Gloucestershire* – and the historical ends are neatly tied in. But it is essentially a library piece. There is no reference to the condition of the mill or of its water-supply, no mention of any machinery being still in place or of the fact that the name, W. Walker and Sons, can still be seen painted in large letters across the front of the building. And its impressive architecture is dismissed in a single sentence.

One cannot, of course, expect all things of all writers and research workers. A more socially-minded kind of investigator would have spent a considerable time trying to discover people who had worked in the mill or who had family memories of it, in order to build up a picture of wages and working conditions. Others would have shown an interest in what the mill produced at different points in its career, in the design and construction of the building, and in the careers of the various owners. And a researcher with a more literary bent might have noted in passing that Dunkirk Mill is reputed to have served as a model for the mill in Mrs. Craik's Victorian novel, *John Halifax, Gentleman*.

Like all other industrial monuments, the English textile mills of the eighteenth and nineteenth centuries appear quite different when they are seen through the eyes of this or that type of specialist. The technical historian is interested only in the machinery, the economic historian only in the facts of ownership and production, the architectural historian only in the appearance of the building. To tour industrial Britain with Sir Nikolaus Pevsner's *Buildings of Britain*, for instance, is to enter a world of permanently uninhabited and unused buildings, cut-outs and models from architectural design books.

In Sir Nikolaus' *Wiltshire* volume (1963, p. 478) for example, we are led into Court Street 'for a first introduction to Trowbridge mills. The older ones of S. Salter's, i.e. those of ashlar, are of *c.* 1814. One has four bays and three storeys and broad four-light wooden windows. Segment-headed windows under the gable. The other is of seven bays and has two-light windows. Then Messrs. Knees', of 1828, two ranges of brick, one of eight bays and four storeys with two-light, segment-headed windows, the other of eleven bays and five storeys with the same type of windows.'

Most people who go in for industrial archaeology in their spare time find it difficult and even absurd to divide knowledge into such water-tight compartments, and there is no reason why they should, since they are, with rare exceptions, working neither for an examination nor for money. The opportunities of getting into print at all are, in fact, confined nowadays almost entirely to the publications of industrial archaeology groups themselves, which is a very good reason for belonging to such a group, although many people are well content to see the results of their labours preserved as a typescript in a library or record office, where anyone with similar interests can consult it. This public-spirited practice is fortunately becoming increasingly common and it is greatly to be encouraged.

Between 1964 and 1974 the quarterly journal, *Industrial Archaeology*, provided an outlet for individuals and groups who wanted to make their work more widely known, but a study of the files of this periodical shows very clearly that the majority of the articles were written by academics of one kind and another and that lesser mortals had to be content with a column or two in the section devoted to 'Notes'. For this reason, the disappearance of *Industrial Archaeology*, which one hopes is only temporary, has probably hit the professionals more than the amateurs.

By no means all local societies produce a journal or bulletin. Where they do, the standard is usually high. In some cases, such as the Bristol Society, it is remarkably high, although one observes over the years that the contributions appear to come from the same small group of active members. This, however, can be an illusion, since the fieldwork and research behind an article may well have been carried out by several people working together and the writing of the article in its final form entrusted to someone practised in the craft.

The editor of such a journal will, inevitably, leave his own stamp on what is published. A scholarly, sober-minded editor is unlikely to publish articles which are not scholarly or sober-minded; a socially-minded editor will put an emphasis on socially-minded contributions; an editor who sets great store by statistics will make sure that there are plenty of statistics. A comparison between two society journals makes this very clear.

BIAS Journal has a scholarly editor and this is reflected on every page of the contents. What one might describe as the BIAS style is well illustrated in a useful article by D. G. Tucker, published in the *BIAS Journal* in 1972 (Vol. 5, p. 15) on 'The Beginnings of Electricity Supply in Bristol, 1889–1902'.

'The public street lighting', we learn from this, 'commenced in November 1893 and provided for 108 arc lamps. Of these, 12 were a.c. arcs connected either two in series across 105V or four in series across 210V. 96 arcs were d.c., operated in eight strings of 12, on the d.c. mains which were supplied at 650V from two 80 amp dynamos. The d.c. cables were, of course, distinct from the a.c. mains and were single-conductor armoured cables laid in the trenches, with twin-conductor unarmoured cables up the lamp posts. A series string of 12 lamps was, of course, very vulnerable to failure, since if any one of the arcs failed to strike, none could. Thus on each route two cables were laid, with lamps connected alternately to one cable or the other; a failure would then leave alternate lamps alight. This scheme also provided an economy measure, since alternate lamps could be extinguished after a certain late hour of night.'

This article is authoritative and clearly written and it almost certainly tells many of its readers a good deal that they did not previously know. But, to anyone with a well-developed sense of mental curiosity, it raises as many questions as it answers. Who, for instance, made the cables? What did they look like and what materials were used? Where and how did the electricians and cable-layers learn their job? How were they recruited and how much were they paid? What sort of accidents occurred? All this information comes within the scope of an article called 'The Beginnings of Electricity Supply in Bristol', yet to have included it here would have made the article far too long to publish, even if the author's tastes and abilities had taken him in the direction of that kind of research. This is an economic, quite as much as an editorial problem. With printing and publishing costs increasing all the time, the day of the long article is over. All writing nowadays has to be pared down and compressed to the point at which the reader has to concentrate very hard in order to follow what is being said. Readability has more and more to be sacrificed to cost. The good note, in such a situation, will be preferred to the good article and, as the American Society for Industrial Archaeology has shown in its superbly well-edited, well-designed and well-printed *Newsletter*, an enormous amount of information can be given in four or six pages, if the editor knows his job and is really interested in communication.

It seems very probable that in the future most communication between industrial archaeologists will take one of three forms – in addition, of course, to that old-fashioned but still useful method of contact known as the letter. There will be the newsletter or bulletin, there will be the exhibition and there will be the illustrated talk or lecture. As many societies are finding to their benefit, a talk can cover a lot of ground very cheaply, a summary of a talk can be duplicated and circulated without too much trouble and expense, and slides are an excellent record of what has been observed. For the time being, at least, the printed word may have almost priced itself out of the market and we may need to re-discover the skills of oral expression, which will be no bad thing.

It is still necessary, unfortunately, to remind many speakers, including even some of considerable experience, that there is a vast difference between the spoken and the printed word. The read lecture is rarely satisfactory, and can be a disaster. The method most likely to succeed is to speak from very brief notes or from mere headings. The paper which is really written for publication and read to an audience on its way, as it were, from the author to the printer is something of an absurdity. The needs of the two occasions are totally different.

There is a strict limit to the quantity of information which the human ear can absorb within ten minutes, an hour, or whatever the allocated time may be. One main point each five minutes is a generous ration. The speaker who floods his audience with facts is rarely popular, and usually unintelligible, although in print his method may be excellent.

Industrial archaeology is essentially visual, and a non-illustrated talk about it is a curiosity. To any speaker who really knows his subject, his slides are his notes, and if they are clear and well chosen they will almost certainly make much more impact than his unassisted words would have done. But there should not be too many of them. For a lecture lasting an hour – and no lecture should last more than an hour – twenty slides should be regarded as the maximum. It is infuriating and frustrating for an audience to be taken through the last ten slides at a gallop, with little explanation of what they are about and sad regrets from the lecturer that his time is so limited.

Much the easiest form of photography is slides, which, under today's commercial conditions, means colour slides. These store easily and are an effective way of illustrating a talk. But it is not easy or cheap to make good black and white prints from them, certainly not of the quality which would be required for reproduction in a book or article. If, therefore, there is a possibility that one's photographs may be eventually destined for publication or for some kind of archive, the choice of black and white is inevitable. This, in turn, means that one has to carry two cameras around, one loaded with colour film and the other with black and white. Eventually, no doubt, technical improvements will make this chore unnecessary, but that day has not yet arrived.

Meanwhile, one or two things can usefully be said about the old-fashioned and neglected art of black and white. It needs more skill and care than colour, both in the photography and in the printing. The national centres which produce colour slides from amateurs' film for the most part do an excellent, reliable job and, so far as there can be such a thing as foolproof photography, taking colour slides is it. Black and white photography, however, is by no means foolproof. It demands great attention to contrasts and to lighting, accurate focus and intelligent printing. Anyone who takes a look at the photographs which form part of amateur exhibitions will know all too well that those in colour usually compare badly with colour slides and that those in black and white are frequently horrible. Every industrial archaeology society should make a point of devoting at least one session a year to the techniques of black and white photography.

One of the greatest experts in taking black and white photographs of buildings and machinery, Mr. Harry Milligan, considered that all that stood between most amateurs and good photographs was a shaking hand. Mr. Milligan, who was in charge of the Manchester Photographic Survey for many years, pinned his faith to the tripod. With modern lenses of reasonable aperture, camera-shake, he was certain, was more often than not the cause of the un-sharpness that is usually blamed on the lens or on bad focusing. The tripod, used as a matter of routine, was, he believed, likely to do more to improve the quality of photographs than any other single factor.

It should also be pointed out that this kind of photograph should be taken with practical, rather than aesthetic considerations in mind. The aim is not to achieve a beautiful composition, but to show in as much detail as possible how something looks and, if it happens to be a piece of machinery or equipment, works. The sole virtues of an industrial archaeologist's photograph are that it should be taken from the correct angle at the correct time of day and that it should show clearly what it is supposed to show, and as little else as possible.

There is also an art in tape-recording and interviewing. It is becoming realised more and more that workers' memories of their jobs are an invaluable source of information and an essential complement to what one learns from visiting sites and museums. Often, indeed, a talk with someone who once worked in the place sends one back for a fresh look with a new pair of eyes. Everyone's imagination, left to work on its own, is limited and a guided tour with a man who spent years of his life in a factory can be a stimulating experience. Sometimes it is easiest to let a tape-recorder do the recording, sometimes, especially with a garrulous informant, a notebook is much

Cigarette manufacturing in Bristol.

This is the right kind of factory photograph. It shows the machine, the process and the worker. Yet it means very little without the full range of supporting material which we have been advocating – technical details of the machinery, and an account by the worker of what she is doing and what she feels about it. How hard did she have to work? Could she carry on a conversation while she worked or was the noise level too high? How much did she earn? Was the machine reliable or was it continually breaking down?

And, to assess the importance of our picture, has anyone preserved an example of one of these machines in a museum? Is there, by any chance, a film showing it working?

better. It is only really necessary to keep a tape for archive purposes. It should normally be regarded as a way of taking notes, and the aim should be to get the material on it transcribed and filed away as soon as possible. For collecting the details of techniques and working conditions, the tape is irrelevant, except as a curiosity. If the sound itself is significant, however, as it may be if one wishes to preserve the noise of machinery, the tape should, of course, be kept.

Every fieldworker should aim at organising his work as if he were going to be killed in a road accident the next day. The records of what he has accomplished to date should always be in a form in which they make sense to another person with a knowledge of the subject. Ideally, no doubt, one should write up one's work as one goes along, but in present-day circumstances this is rarely possible. Some superhuman figures accomplish it, nonetheless. The redoubtable Sir Nikolaus Pevsner for many years made a practice of completing, ready for the printer, each evening in his hotel bedroom, the section of the particular *Buildings of Britain* volume on which he had been carrying out fieldwork during the day. Most of us, however, are likely to have to content ourselves with a rather less satisfactory rate of progress.

Sir Nikolaus has always been a words-man, not a pictures-man. If he needed pictures or drawings, they were produced by other people with the appropriate skills. His personal business, as he saw it, was to get the text right and to go to sleep each night up-to-date. There were no sketches and plans to tidy up and re-draw.

The technical requirements for drawings to illustrate papers and notes dealing with industrial archaeology are exactly the same as for archaeology in general. They are admirably set out in *The Preparation of Archaeological Reports* (John Baker, second edition 1974, pp. 34–7) and all that needs to be repeated here is that they should be drawn in Indian ink, either on a transparent plastic or on cartridge paper, that the detail should remain absolutely clear when it is reduced to the actual size needed by the editor, and that the lettering should be first-class. Nothing looks worse, whether in a publication or an exhibition, than shoddy, ill-formed, irregular lettering. If one feels incapable of producing a good, well-lettered drawing oneself – and not everyone has the necessary eye or steadiness of hand – the only answer is to entrust the execution of the finished drawing to an expert, who may be an artist, an

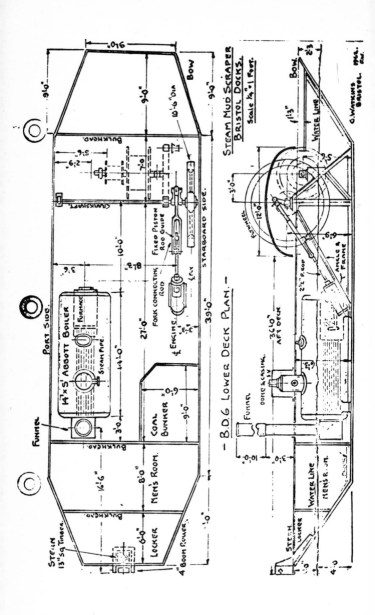

STEAM MUD SCRAPER.
BRISTOL DOCKS.
Scale ¼" = 1 Feet.

— B.D.6 LOWER DECK PLAN. —

G.WATKINS. 1966.
BRISTOL.
Eng.

14"x5" ABBOTT BOILER

FURNACE

STEAM PIPE.

Funnel

Port Side.

Bow

Bulkhead

Crankshaft

Starboard Side.

Fixed Piston
Rod Guide

Fork Connecting
Rod

₵ Engine.

COAL BUNKER

Men's Room.

Locker

Stern 13" Sq Timber.

4" Boom Roller.

Water Line

Funnel

Flywheel

Dome Casing.
Dry

Aft Deck

Angle & T Frame

2½" P. Rod.

Stern
Locker

Water Line

Men's Jn.

Diagram, drawn by George Watkins, of the steam-driven
mud-dredger at the City Docks, Bristol, designed by
Isambard Kingdom Brunel.

*The essential feature of a good sketch-plan is that it shall leave
one in no doubt as to how the piece of equipment worked. By
this criterion, George Watkins' drawing does what is required
of it excellently. It is not, as it stands, particularly elegant, but
it is clear and neat and provides all the information which
would be required to produce a handsome finished drawing on
some other occasion.*

---

architectural or engineering draughtsman, or a geographer
specialising in map work.

But nobody other than the author himself or someone
working closely with him throughout his research and fieldwork is capable of making the necessary measurements, rough
drawings and selection of facts which make up the raw material
of the drawing. Anyone, however lacking in artistic ability, is
capable of handling a tape-measure and of making a first
sketch. For anything beyond this, one has to decide whether
one's time and money are best spent learning and practising
how to draw and letter to an acceptable standard, or whether
it is likely to be quicker and more economic to pay or persuade
an expert to do the job.

A drawing should not be asked to do too much. Some
authors almost write the article on the drawing, with the
inevitable result that it becomes confusing and not infrequently
incomprehensible. A drawing should show something very
simple – the ground plan of a mill, the construction of a
water wheel, the position of a paper-works along a river. A
complicated machine drawing may be easy to follow when full
size, yet virtually useless when brought down to fill a page in a
periodical.

If one happens to be good at making maps and sketches, the
gift can, on occasion, get out of control, so that one forgets the
point of drawings – to clarify some particular point in the
text – and accumulates them for their own sake. The same is
true of statistical diagrams. It is difficult to convince some
authors that a row of figures is much easier to understand than
the ingenious diagram they have worked out to explain the

figures, but so indeed it can be. Diagrams and drawings can become a mere gimmick. Make sure they are there for a genuine purpose.

It is difficult to give any very helpful advice about book publication. Most people who write a book about some aspect of industrial archaeology are, in a sense, professionals. They may be primarily engineers, biographers, economic historians, museum experts, social historians, architects or industrialists, but, whatever their main occupation, it is likely to have a fairly close connection with the book they have decided to write. They will probably know quite a number of people working in the same field as themselves and they will be, to a greater or lesser extent, sensitive to current needs and fashions. This does not necessarily mean, however, that they have an abundance of time in which to write it, nor that they will find it particularly easy to discover a publisher.

Prospective authors do well to realise, however, that publishers are interested only in books which they have reason to believe will sell. Their judgement may occasionally prove to be wrong, of course, and every reputable publisher will admit to having, just once or twice in his career, put out a book for which he saw no real commercial prospects, but which he was proud of publishing, simply because it was a good book.

A book on cotton-mills or steam engines or iron-workings is not in the same position as a novel or a biography or an account of travels in Mexico. It is not well suited to being sent, in typescript, from publisher to publisher in the hope that one of them will see merit and market success in it. There are probably not more than half a dozen British publishers who would see it fitting easily and naturally into their list, and whose eyes would light up at the thought of becoming responsible for it. Even they would want to be well satisfied that the author knew his subject, and the author who has already published one or two substantial articles is in a much stronger position when it comes to getting a book launched. It can also be helpful to be known for one's work in some other medium, say lecturing or broadcasting.

If one has a book of this kind in mind, the wisest plan is always to write to publishers, enclosing a synopsis and a clear statement of the proposed treatment, before one sets pen to paper at all. To write a full-length book, embodying the fruits of a great deal of research, and to go to the not inconsiderable expense of having it typed, and of obtaining suitable photographs and drawings, without a prior contract ensuring publication, is both hazardous and optimistic. If, however, an author is public-spirited to an unusual degree, he may be willing to deposit his manuscript with a public library, having failed to find a publisher for it, but this is not a plan of action one can recommend in advance.

Section Four

Museums, libraries and archives

One discovers the strong and weak points of a library or a museum only by working, or attempting to work, in it. An establishment which appears interesting, friendly and efficient to the casual visitor can prove very different when one has occasion really to test its facilities and, equally frequently, somewhere which on the surface gives the impression of having little to offer may turn out to be a gold-mine, once the staff has a chance to dig into cupboards, stores and files. A major problem all over the country, however, is that many of the places one wants to use are not open in the evenings or at weekends. In most cases, but not all, this is caused by a shortage of money. The budget will not allow curators to do many of the things they would like to do and which they know should be done, and in Britain's present impoverished state one simply has to accept this. It is, none the less, infuriating to know that the material one desperately needs to use is lying there month by month, not being consulted by anyone, while a more than willing customer is forced to earn a living during the hours when the public is allowed access to the collection. Even so, it is always worthwhile to make a friend of the person in charge. Facilities which the rules and regulations say are impossible can often be arranged discreetly and privately, and often are. Official restrictions exist to be overcome and, generally speaking, the smaller the institution, the easier it is to arrive at a quiet understanding. The big museums and libraries are the ones where the rules tend to be exactly what they say, and where the doors are locked and unlocked at the hours stated on the brass plate.

This principle should be kept closely in mind when consulting the lists which follow, with the additional piece of advice that privately-owned institutions usually find it possible to be more flexible than those run by local authorities and government departments.

One may, perhaps, be permitted to note as a matter of national pride, that Britain has by far the largest number and most comprehensive range in the world of museums devoted to industry and technology.

It can be assumed that all these museums maintain collections of books, pamphlets, photographs and other pictorial material. A number also collect tapes and films.

The general museums of science, technology and industry

Co. Durham

The North of England Open-Air Museum, Beamish Hall, Stanley
The aim of this museum is to show how previous generations of people in the North-East have lived and earned a living. Old industrial buildings and machines have been installed on the 200 acre site and particular attention has been paid to railways and road transport. An indoor museum in Beamish Hall itself presents the broad pattern of development in the region.
Opening times Daily ex. M and including Bank Holidays. Easter–end of September, 10–6 (last admission 5). Oct.–Easter F., Sa., Su. 10–5 (last admission 4).

Cumbria

Museum of Lakeland Life and Industry, Abbot Hall, Kendal, LA9 5AL
Industries and life in the region, with special reference to agriculture, mining, shipping and railways.
Opening times M–F 10.30–12.30, 2–5; Sa., Su. 2–5. Closed two weeks at Christmas.

Derbyshire

Derby Museum of Industry and Technology, The Silk Mill, Silk Mill Lane, off Full Street, Derby
The industries of Derby and the surrounding region. Textiles, Rolls-Royce and locomotive building are especially well covered.
Opening times Tu.–F 10–5.45; Sa. 10–4.45. Closed Good F, Christmas Day, Boxing Day and New Year's Day.

Greater Manchester

North-Western Museum of Science and Industry, 97 Grosvenor Street, Manchester, M1 7HF

Scientific equipment and machines, especially examples connected with the North-West. Documents, drawings and photographs from local industrial and transport concerns, including Beyer Peacock.

Opening times M–Sa. 10–5. Easter, Spring and Late Summer Bank Holidays 10–5. Closed Christmas Day, Boxing Day, Good F and 'certain days at the New Year' (ask locally for details).

Leicestershire

Museum of Technology for the East Midlands, Abbey Pumping Station, Corporation Road, Leicester

Imaginatively housed in the former Abbey Sewage Pumping Station. The strong points at the moment are hosiery, road vehicles and steam engines, with a great deal of material of all kinds still in store and viewable only by prior arrangement.

Opening times M–Sa. 10–5.30; Su. 2–5.30.

London

The Science Museum, Exhibition Road, London SW7 2DD

The nation's filing cabinet of technical material. Beloved of school parties, and, for this reason, adults often find it a rather noisy place. It covers the full range, from steam engines to kitchen stoves and from dyestuffs to space travel. Many of its problems are due to an appalling and chronic shortage of space, which is a disgrace to a country claiming to be civilised. There is a strong publications section and the introductory booklets to various special subjects, such as the steam engine, are excellent value.

Opening times M–Sa. 10–6; Su. 2.30–6. Closed Good F, Christmas Eve, Christmas Day, Boxing Day and New Year's Day.

Norfolk

Bridewell Museum of Local Industries and Rural Crafts, Bridewell Alley, St. Andrew's Street, Norwich, NR2 1AQ

A small, well-arranged museum devoted to the Norwich area, with an emphasis on the agriculture-based industries

and river and coastal shipping. Excellent photographic collection.
Opening times Weekdays 10–5.

Nottinghamshire

Nottingham Industrial Museum, Courtyard Buildings, Wollaton Park, Nottingham, NG8 2AE
The range of Nottingham's industries, especially bicycles and motorcycles and lace.
Opening times Apr.–Sept., Th. and Sa. 10–6.45. Oct. and Mar., Th. and Sa. 10–5.15. Nov.–Feb., Th. and Sa. 10–dusk. Su., Mar.–Oct. 2–4.45; Nov.–Feb. 1.30–dusk.

Shropshire

Ironbridge Gorge Museum Trust, Offices: Southside, Church Hill, Ironbridge, Telford, Shropshire, TF8 7RE
An open-air museum, created around monuments of the first Industrial Revolution. The exhibits are concerned particularly with coal, iron, porcelain and canal transport.
Opening times Daily except Christmas Day, Apr.–Oct. 10–6; Nov.–Mar. 10–5.

Tyne and Wear

Museum of Science and Engineering, Exhibition Park, Great North Road, Newcastle upon Tyne, NE2 2PZ
Industries and transport of the Newcastle area, with an emphasis on shipbuilding, railways and shipping.
Opening times M–F 9.30–6; Sa. 9.30–4; Su. 3–5. Bank Holidays 10–5.

West Midlands

Museum of Science and Industry, Newhall Street, Birmingham, B3 1RZ
Scientific principles and applications. History of the industries of the West Midlands. Steam engines regularly run on steam.
Opening times M–F 10–5; Sa. 10–5.30; Su. 2–5.30. 1st W in month 10–9. Closed Good F, Christmas Day and Boxing Day.

The Black Country Museum, Tipton Road, Dudley
The industry, transport and social history of the Black Country.
Opening times M–Sa. 10–6.

Yorkshire (West)

Bradford Industrial Museum, Moorside Mills, Moorside Road, Bradford, BD2 3HP

The industrial history of the Bradford region, with an emphasis on woollen textiles, road and railway transport and engineering.

Opening times   M–Sa. 10–6; Su. 2–5.

Ireland, Northern

Ulster Museum, Department of Industry and Technology, Botanic Gardens, Belfast, BT9 5AB

Industrial development of Northern Ireland.

Opening times   M–Sa. 11–6; Su. 2.30–5.30.

Scotland

Royal Scottish Museum, Department of Technology, Chambers Street, Edinburgh, EH1 1JF

Science and its applications. Scottish industries, especially mining, metal-working, engineering, aircraft and transport.

Opening times   M–Sa. 10–5; Su. 2–5. Closed Christmas Day and January 1–2.

Wales

National Museum of Wales, Department of Industry, Cathays Park, Cardiff, Gwent, CF1 3NP

History of Welsh industries, especially mining, iron and steel, shipping and quarrying.

Opening times   Oct.–Mar., weekdays 10–5. Apr.–Sept., including Bank Holidays and Tu. following, weekdays 10–6; Su. 2.30–5. Closed Christmas Eve, Christmas Day, Boxing Day, New Year's Day and Good F.

The Industrial Museum, Royal Institution of South Wales, Victoria Road, Swansea, West Glamorgan

Industrial and transport development of South Wales.

Opening times   M–Sa., Bank Holidays 10–5.

Transport Museums

There are almost, one is tempted to say, too many transport museums, and the owners and curators of a few of them could usefully be reminded that four horse-drawn carriages or two railway engines, four coaches and a stretch of track do not in themselves constitute a museum, although they may with proper presentation make the core of a museum. But there are, perhaps unfortunately, no patent rights in the word 'museum' and as museums are, as yet, unaffected by the Trade Descriptions Act, the consumer can only learn to defend himself against over-ambitious selling.

To discourage sectarianism and unbecoming arrogance among railway – and aeroplane – enthusiasts, museums devoted to road, rail, water and air transport are grouped together in the list which follows.

Avon

S.S. 'Great Britain', Great Western Dock, Gas Ferry Road, off Cumberland Road, Bristol
Brunel's great iron ship (1843), now under restoration in the dock where she was originally built.
Opening times Daily, Apr.–Oct. 10–6; Nov.–Mar. 10–5.
Dodington Carriage Museum, Dodington, Chipping Sodbury
Horse-drawn vehicles, in a former coach-house and stable complex. Harness and saddlery. Library relating to carriages and coaching.
Opening times March 22–Sept. 28, M–Su. 11–5.30.

Bedfordshire

The Shuttleworth Collection, Old Warden Aerodrome, Biggleswade
Flyable old aircraft. Road vehicles.
Opening times Daily 10–5. Closed Christmas Eve, Christmas Day, Boxing Day.

Buckinghamshire

Quainton Railway Museum, Railway Station, Quainton, Aylesbury
A working steam museum in the old goods yard and station. Locomotives. Railway equipment and relics.
Opening times Spring and summer weekends, as announced locally.

Cambridgeshire

Duxford Airfield, near Duxford

One of the oldest surviving groups of aircraft hangars in the country now houses the main reserve collection of large exhibits – aircraft and artillery vehicles – from the Imperial War Museum. Exhibition of photographs also.

Opening times   To be announced in 1976.

Cleveland

Hartlepool Maritime Museum, Northgate, Hartlepool, TS24 0LT

Shipbuilding, marine engineering, fishing.

Opening times   M–Sa. 10–5.

Stockton and Darlington Railway Museum, Bridge Street, Stockton-on-Tees

In the world's first railway booking office. Early railway material, with special reference to the Stockton and Darlington Railway.

Opening times   M–Sa. 10–6.

Cornwall

Great Western Society, Bodmin Depot, Hanleigh Road, Bodmin

Two GWR locomotives and items of GWR rolling stock.

Opening times   Su. 2–5.

Co. Durham

Darlington Museum, Tubwell Row, Darlington, DL1 1PD

History of the Stockton and Darlington Railway.

Opening times   M–W, F 10–1, 2–6; Th. 10–1; Sa. 10–1, 2–5.30. Bank Holidays 10–1, 2–6.

Darlington North Road Station Museum, North Road, Darlington

Fully restored station (1842) on original route of Stockton and Darlington Railway. Locomotives, rolling stock and supporting displays.

Opening times   As for Darlington Museum

Derbyshire

The Donington Collection, Donington Park, Castle Donington, Derby

Racing cars. History of motor-racing.

Opening times   Daily 10–6.

Tramway Museum, Cliff Quarry, Crich, Matlock, DE4 5DP
Representative collection of tramcars from Britain and overseas, 1873–1953. Depots. Workshops. Operating tramway.
Opening times Easter–Oct., Sa., Su., Bank Holidays, 11–dusk (or 7.30). June–Aug. also Tu.–Th. 10–5.

Dinting Railway Centre, Dinting Lane, Glossop
Operating steam centre, with large collection of locomotives.
Opening times Sa., Su., Bank Holidays, 10.30–5.

Devon

South Devon Railway Museum, Dawlish Warren Station, Dawlish
Railway relics. Documents. Photographs. Operating model railway.
Opening times Spring Bank Holiday–Sept. 30 10–dusk.

Exeter Maritime Museum, The Quay, Exeter, EX2 4AN
In eighteenth century canal warehouse and canal basin. Sailing ships from all over the world. Steam tug. Brunel dredger.
Opening times Daily, including Bank Holidays, 10–6. Closed Christmas Day, Boxing Day.

Torbay Aircraft Museum, Higher Blagdon, near Paignton TQ3 3YG
Aircraft. Engines. Armament. Relics. Photographs. Documents.
Opening times Summer 10–6. Winter daily 10–4. Closed Christmas Day and Boxing Day.

Schooner 'Kathleen and May', Sutton Harbour, Barbican, Plymouth
The former trading schooner contains a National Maritime Museum display relating to the history of British coastal sailing ships.
Opening times Easter–Oct. 31 daily 11–6.

Totnes Motor Museum, Totnes
Motor cars, 1920s onwards.
Opening times Easter–Oct. 31 daily 10–6.

Essex

Historic Aircraft Museum, Aviation Way, Southend, S52 6UL
Thirty restored aircraft, with several in flying condition.
Opening times June–Sept. daily 9–7. Oct.–May, Sa, Su. 10–5.

Gloucestershire

Skyfame Aircraft Museum, Staverton Airport, Cheltenham
Aircraft, mostly 1939 onwards. Engines. Equipment.
Opening times Daily 11–5.

Dean Forest Railway Preservation Society Museum, The Station, Parkend
Standard gauge locomotives and rolling stock. Railway equipment, and relics. Photographs. Documents.
Opening times M–F by appointment. Sa., Su., Bank Holidays 2–6. Special Open Days by local announcement.

Dowty Railway Preservation Society, Northway Lane, Ashchurch, near Tewkesbury
Locomotives and rolling stock.
Opening times Su., Bank Holidays 2–6. Closed Christmas and New Year.

Winchcombe Railway Museum, 23 Gloucester Street, Winchcombe
Signals and associated equipment. Permanent way equipment. Tickets and documents.
Opening times Bank Holidays and summer Sundays 2.30–dusk.

Greater Manchester

Bury Transport Museum, Castlecroft Road, Bury, BL9 0LN
The headquarters of the East Lancashire Railway Preservation Society. Steam locomotives. Rolling stock. Signalling and other equipment. Buses and other road vehicles.
Opening times Sa., Su., Bank Holidays 11–5.

Stockport Aircraft Preservation Society Museum, 27 Barnfield Road East, Woodsmoor, Stockport, and Handforth Hangar No. 31
Complete aircraft and sections. Aviation library, with drawings and production histories available on loan.
Opening times July–Aug., Sa., Su. 10–6. Other times by appointment.

The Aeroplane Collection Limited, 8 Greenfield Avenue, Urmston
Aircraft and associated items, many of which are at present on loan to other museums. Photographic library. Technical and general aviation literature dating back to the early days of flying.
Opening times By appointment.

Hampshire

Buckler's Hard Maritime Museum, Buckler's Hard, Beaulieu, SO4 7ZN

History of the eighteenth century shipbuilding village and of the ships that were built there. Nelson relics.

Opening times Oct.–Easter, daily 10–4.30. Easter–Spring Bank Holiday, daily 10–6. Spring Bank Holiday–Sept., daily 10–9.

National Motor Museum, Palace House, Beaulieu, SO4 7ZN

Collections of vehicles and equipment illustrating the development of motoring from 1895 to the present day.

Opening times Oct.–Easter, daily 10–5. Easter–Sept., daily 10–6.30 (10–8.30 during August).

Breamore Carriage Museum, Breamore House, near Fordingbridge

In the seventeenth century stables of Breamore House. Horse-drawn vehicles and equipment from 1800.

Opening times Good F–Sept. 30, Tu–Th., Sa., Su., Bank Holidays 2–5.30.

Hereford and Worcester

Bulmer Railway Centre, Whitecross Road, Hereford

Steam and diesel locomotives, including 'King George V', with its own set of Pullman coaches. Wagons. Coaches.

Opening times Apr.–Sept., Sa., Su. 2–5.

Hertfordshire

de Havilland Mosquito Aircraft Museum, Salisbury Hall, London Colney, near St. Albans.

Mosquito and other wooden aircraft. Mosquito relics and photographs. Jet engines.

Opening times Easter Su.–Sept. 10.30–5.30, including Bank Holidays. July–Sept. also Th. 10.30–5.30.

Humberside (North)

Transport and Archaeology Museum, 36 High Street, Kingston-upon-Hull

Horse-drawn vehicles. Cars and motorcycles. Cycles. Trams. Locomotives.

Opening times M–Sa. 10–5; Su. 2.30–4.30. Closed Christmas Day, Boxing Day, Good F.

Kent

South Eastern Steam Centre, Hunter Avenue, Ashford
Standard-gauge locomotives and rolling stock, including Pullman cars.
Opening times May–Oct., Easter M and 2nd Su. of each month 11–5.

The Longfield Collection, 'The Sidings', 193 Main Road, Longfield, Dartford
Steam, diesel, petrol and paraffin narrow-gauge locomotives.
Opening times By appointment.

Tyrwhitt-Drake Museum of Carriages, Archbishop's Stables, Mill Street, Maidstone
Collection illustrating the development of horse-drawn transport and of coachbuilding.
Opening times Weekdays 10–1, 2–5. Closed Bank Holidays.

Historic Vehicle Collection of Mr. C. M. Booth, Falstaff Antiques, High Street, Rolvenden, TN17 4LP
Three-wheel cars. Light vans. Bicycles. Early motoring relics. Signs. Posters. Photographs.
Opening times M–Sa. 10–6 (W 10–1). Other times by arrangement.

Lancashire

Steamtown Railway Museum, Warton Road, Carnforth
GWR, LMSR, LNER, SR and industrial locomotives dating from 1908.
Opening times Daily 9–6.

The Royal Umpire Exhibition, Croston, near Leyland
Horse-drawn carriages and coaches and their equipment.
Opening times Easter–Oct. 9–9.

Lytham Motive Power Museum, Dock Road, Lytham
Standard and narrow gauge locomotives and rolling stock dating from 1887. Vintage cars.
Opening times May–Oct., Tu–Th., Sa., Su. 11–5.

Leicestershire

Museum of the Great Central Railway (Main Line Steam Trust Ltd.) 13 New Street, Leicester, and Loughborough Central Station
Main-line and industrial locomotives. Goods and passenger rolling stock. Operating steam trains.
Opening times Sa., Su., Bank Holidays 11–6.30.

Museum of Technology for the East Midlands: Railway Museum, London Road, Stoneygate, Leicester
Four locomotives and items of local railway history.
Opening times Th.–Su. 2–5.30.

Percy Pilcher Museum, Stanford Hall, Lutterworth
Full-size replica of Percy Pilcher's Flying Machine of 1898, in which he was killed at Stanford in 1899. Documents relating to Pilcher and his experiments. Photographs of his flights and machines.
Opening times Easter–Sept., Th., Sa., Su. 2.30–6. Bank Holidays 12–6.

Stanford Hall Motorcycle and Car Museum, Lutterworth
Motorcycles, cars and bicycles.
Opening times Easter–Sept., Th., Sa., Su. 2.30–6. Bank Holidays 12–6.

Museum of Shackerstone Railway Society Ltd., Shackerstone Station, near Market Bosworth
Steam, diesel and petrol locomotives. Rolling stock. Railway relics.
Opening times Su., Bank Holidays 11–6.

Lincolnshire

Museum of the Lincolnshire Vintage Vehicle Society, Whisby Road, North Hykeham
Vintage cars, buses, lorries.
Opening times May–Sept., 2nd S. of each month 2–5.

Lincolnshire Aviation Museum, Old Railway Yard, Tattershall
Small aircraft. Aero-engines. Cockpit sections. Photographs and aeronautical relics.
Opening times Su., Bank Holidays 11–6.

London

London Transport Collection, Syon Park, Brentford
Buses, trams, trolley-buses, locomotives and rolling stock used by London Transport.
Opening times Apr.–Sept. 10–7. Oct.–Mar. 10–5.

World of Motoring Exhibition, Syon Park, Brentford
History of motoring shown in a series of montages.
Opening times M–Sa. 9–5.30; Su., Bank Holidays 10–5. Closed Christmas Day, Boxing Day.

London General Cab Company Museum, 1–3 Brixton Road, Brixton, London SW9
Development of the London taxi.
Opening times   M–F 8–5.

Royal Air Force Museum, Hendon, London NW9 5LL
Development of military aviation, 1870 onwards. Library of books, documents, photographs.
Opening times   M–Sa. 10–6; Su. 2–6. Closed Good F, Dec. 24–26.

National Maritime Museum, Romney Road, London SE10 9NF
British shipbuilding and shipping from the sixteenth century onwards. Library of books, manuscripts, charts, photographs.
Opening times   Weekdays 10–6; Su. 2.30–6. Closed Dec. 24–26, New Year's Day and Good F.

Norfolk

Caister Castle Motor Museum, Caister-on-Sea
Steam and internal combustion road vehicles, 1896 onwards.
Opening times   Mid May–Sept., daily 10.30–5.

Bressingham Steam Museum, Diss
Standard and narrow-gauge locomotives, operating on tracks. Traction and other steam-powered road vehicles.
Opening times   Th. 1.30–5.30; Su. and Bank Holidays, 1.30–6.

Maritime Museum for East Anglia, Marine Parade, Great Yarmouth
East Anglian maritime history, including the Norfolk Wherry.
Opening times   June–Sept., daily 10–1, 2–8. Oct.–May, M–F 10–1, 2–5.30.

The Norfolk Wherry 'Albion', Norfolk Wherry Trust, Scoutbush, Hoveton, Norwich
The *Albion* (1898) is the only Norfolk Trading Wherry still under sail. She has been restored and is open to the public.
Opening times   By arrangement.

Sandringham Motor Museum, Sandringham Estate
The Motor Museum forms part of a general museum complex. The Royal Daimler cars used by members of the Royal Family. Photographs of Royal cars and Royal motorists.
Opening times   Apr., May, Sept., Tu.–Th. 11–5. June, July,

Aug., Tu.–F 11–5. Easter Su. and M, Spring Bank Holiday and last Su. and M in May 11–5.

North Norfolk Railways Museum, Sheringham Station, Sheringham

Operating steam trains. Rolling stock, including two Directors' Saloons. Railway relics, with an emphasis on items formerly in use on East Anglian railways.

Opening times Easter–Oct., daily 10–6.

Northamptonshire

Waterways Museum, Stoke Bruerne, near Towcester, NN12 7SE

British canal history, with boats, equipment, paintings and photographs. Library of documents and photographs.

Opening times Apr.–1st week in Oct., daily 10–6. 2nd week in Oct.–Mar., Tu.–Su. 10–4. Closed Christmas Day, Boxing Day.

Oxfordshire

Great Western Society Museum, Didcot Engine Shed, Didcot

Large collection of GWR locomotives and rolling stock, and the Wantage tram, *Shannon* (1857), the oldest engine in the British Isles still steamed.

Opening times 11–5 on these days: Su., Easter–Sept.; M of Easter, Spring and Late Summer Bank Holidays; daily June 29–July 6 and August 3–10.

Shropshire

Severn Valley Railway, Bridgnorth

Operates passenger service between Bridgnorth and Hampton. Collection of locomotives and rolling stock on view at Bridgnorth and Bewdley.

Opening times Mar.–Oct. 10–6.

Somerset

Cheddar Motor and Transport Museum, The Cliffs, Cheddar, BS27 3QA

Cars and motorcycles dating from 1898. Tricycles. Motoring accessories.

Opening times Apr.–Sept., daily 10–dusk. Oct.–Mar. 10–4. Closed Christmas Day.

Somerset and Dorset Railway Museum, Radstock North Station, Radstock

Locomotives, rolling stock and equipment from the former Somerset and Dorset and related railways.

Opening times Mar.–Oct., Last Sa., Su. of each month 11–5; other weekends, Su. 11–5.

East Somerset Railway Museum, Cranmore, Shepton Mallet

Large collection of locomotives and rolling stock.

Opening times Daily 9–6.

Fleet Air Arm Museum, Royal Naval Air Station, Yeovilton, near Ilchester

Naval aviation from 1910 to the present day. Aircraft. Engines. Flying clothing. Photographs.

Opening times M–Sa. 10–5.30; Su. 12.30–5.30.

Suffolk

East Anglia Transport Museum, Chapel Road, Carlton Colville, Lowestoft

All forms of mechanical land transport. Operational tramway and a narrow-gauge railway.

Opening times May 24–Sept. 30, Sa. 2–4. May 25–Sept. 30, Su. and Bank Holidays, 11–6.

Surrey

Cobham Bus Museum, Redhill Road, Cobham

A collection of forty old buses and coaches and related equipment, formed by the London Bus Preservation Group.

Opening times By appointment.

Tyne and Wear

Monkwearmouth Station Museum, North Bridge Street, Sunderland, SR5 1AR

The central feature of the Museum is the Edwardian booking office, but the main station building is 1848. The collections show the history of local land transport, by means of models, paintings, photographs, uniforms and equipment.

Opening times M–F 9.30–5.30; Sa. 9.30–4. Bank Holiday M 10–5.

Warwickshire

Stratford Motor Museum, 1 Shakespeare Street, Stratford-on-Avon

Grand touring cars. Motorcycles. Replica of a garage of the 1920s.
Opening times   Daily 10.30–6.

West Midlands

Birmingham Railway Museum, The Steam Depot, Warwick Road, Tyseley
Steam locomotives, mostly GWR and LMS. Pullman and other coaches. Maintenance depot and engineering workshops for preserved locomotives.
Opening times   Apr.–Oct., Su. 2–5.30. Other times by arrangement.

Aerospace Museum, RAF Cosford, Wolverhampton
Historic military aircraft. Aero-engines. Rockets.
Opening times   Apr.–Oct., 1st Su. in each month 1.30–5.

Wiltshire

Great Western Railway Museum, Faringdon Road, Swindon
Historic GWR locomotives. Operating equipment. Models. Posters. Tickets.
Opening times   M–Sa., Bank Holidays, 10–5; Su. 2–5.

Yorkshire (North)

Yorkshire Museum of Horse-Drawn Transport, York Mills, Aysgarth Falls, near Hawes
A collection of about fifty horse-drawn vehicles of all types, housed in a former woollen mill, which once produced the red cloth for Garibaldi's army uniforms.
Opening times   Easter–Oct., daily 10–6.

National Railway Museum, Leeman Road, York, YO2 4XJ
History and development of railway engineering. Social and economic aspects of railway history. Locomotives. Rolling stock. Signalling and permanent way equipment. Display and reference collections of paintings, posters, photographs, drawings and films.
Opening times   M–Sa. 10–6; Su. 2.30–6. Closed Dec. 24–26, Jan. 1, Good F.

Yorkshire (South)

Sandtoft Transport Centre, Hatfield, Doncaster
Forty trolley-buses, sometimes operating. Buses.
Opening times   Easter–Oct., Sa., Su. 10–6.

Yorkshire (West)

Tolson Memorial Museum, Ravensknowle Park, Wakefield Road, Huddersfield

Horse-drawn vehicles. Cycles. Tri-cars, made in Huddersfield.

Opening times M–Sa., Bank Holidays, 10.30–5; Su. 2–5.

Keighley and Worth Valley Railway Museum, Haworth, Keighley

The Museum forms part of the Keighley and Worth Valley Railway. It contains thirty-five steam locomotives and three diesel-electric, together with two diesel rail buses, and covers the period 1874–1956.

Opening times Sa., Public Holidays, 8–dusk; Su. 10–dusk.

Channel Islands

Jersey Motor Museum, St. Peter's Village, Jersey

Motorcars and motorcycles from *c.* 1900 onwards. Jersey steam-railway relics.

Opening times Apr.–Nov., daily 10–5.

Isle of Man

Castletown Nautical Museum, Bridge Street, Castletown

Schooner-rigged yacht, 'Peggy'. Sail-maker's loft. Ship models. Photographs. Documents.

Opening times Mid June–late Sept., weekdays 10–1, 2–5.

Manx Motor Museum, Crosby

Steam and petrol-driven cars.

Opening times M–Sa. 10–5.

Murray's Motorcycle Museum, Bungalow Corner, Snaefell Mountain T.T. Course

Veteran and vintage motorcycles. Photographs and other items of motorcycling lore.

Opening times Easter–Sept., daily 10–5.

Ireland, Northern

Belfast Transport Museum, Witham Street, Newtownards Road, Belfast

Horse-drawn vehicles. Steam locomotives. Railway rolling stock. Horse, steam and electric trams. Cars and motor-

cycles. Cycles. Ship models.
Opening times Weekdays 10–6; W 10–9.
North West of Ireland Railway Society Museum, 6 Victoria Road, Londonderry
Locomotives, railcars and operating equipment from Irish railways.
Opening times Sa. 10.30–12.30, 2.30–4.30.

Ireland, Republic of

Mount Usher Museum, Ashford, Co. Wicklow
Eighteenth- and nineteenth-century carriages, made by coachbuilders in Dublin, Gorey, Newtownards and London.
Opening times May–Sept., M–Sa. 10–6; Su. 2.30–5.30. Oct.–Apr., M–Sa. 10–5.
Celbridge Motor Museum, Temple Mills House, Celbridge, Co. Kildare
Vintage motorcars and motorcycles. Steam engine models.
Opening times By appointment.

Scotland (Central)

Doune Motor Museum, Carse of Cambus, Doune, Perthshire
Lord Doune's collection of vintage and veteran cars.
Opening times Apr.–Oct., daily 10–6.

Scotland (Fife)

Lochty Private Railway Museum, Lochty Farm, Cupar–Crail Road
Locomotives and rolling stock formerly used on Scottish lines. Industrial locomotives.
Opening times Su. 2–5.

Scotland (Lothians)

Myreton Motor Museum, Aberlady
Commercial and military vehicles. Motorcycles. Bicycles. Tractors.
Opening times Oct.–Easter, Sa., Su. 10–5. Easter–Oct., daily 10–6.
Edinburgh City Transport Museum, Shrubhill Depot, Leith Walk, Edinburgh, EH7 4PA
Horse and electric trams and buses used in Edinburgh.
Opening times M–Sa., Bank Holidays 10–5.

Scotland (Strathclyde)

Glasgow Museum of Transport, 25 Albert Drive, Glasgow, G41 2PE
In former Corporation Tramcar Works. Horse-drawn vehicles. Motorcars. Cycles and motorcycles. Locomotives.
Opening times M–Sa., Bank Holidays 10–5; Su. 2–5. Closed Christmas Day, January 1.

Scotland (Tayside)

Strathallan Aircraft Collection, Strathallan Airfield, Auchterader, Perthshire, PH3 1LA
Aircraft, mainly 1939–45.
Opening times M–F 10–5; Sa., Su., Bank Holidays 10–dusk.

Wales (Dyfed)

Pembrokeshire Motor Museum, Royal Garrison Theatre, Pembroke Dock
Cycles, motorcycles, lorries and cars from 1860, including accessories, clothing, tools.
Opening times Easter–Sept., daily 10–6.

Wales (Gwynedd)

Conwy Valley Railway Museum, Old Goods Yard, Betws-y-coed
Vehicles from the Conwy Valley Railway, 1895 onwards. Equipment and relics from the North Wales railways.
Opening times Daily 10.30–5 (until 7 during July–Aug. and on Bank Holidays).

Corris Railway Museum, Corris Station Yard, Corris
Small exhibits and photographs relating to the Corris Railway.
Opening times Announced locally.

Narrow Gauge Railway Museum, Towyn
Associated with the Talyllyn Railway. Locomotives, rolling stock and other items from British narrow-gauge railways.
Opening times Easter–Oct., daily 10–5. Other times by appointment.

Museums illustrating the history of particular industries

Most local and regional museums have sections dealing with the major industries of the area. Those which follow are concerned entirely or mainly with a particular industry.

It will be noticed that many important industries either have no museum at all devoted to them, or are given a quite inadequate amount of attention. We have, for instance, no museums of stone-quarrying, brick and tile-making, paper, oil, synthetic fibres, chemicals, plastics, baking, machine-tools, printing, rubber, distilling or gas, and quite inadequate museum treatment of brewing, electricity-generation and transmission, shipbuilding, milling and automobile production. This list is as significant for its omissions as for what is included.

Clocks, watches

Morath Bros. Museum, 71 Dale Street, Liverpool, Merseyside
A company museum. Clocks.
Opening times Weekdays 2–5.

Clothing, footwear

Symington Museum of Period Corsetry, R. and W. H. Symington and Co., P.O. Box 5, Market Harborough, Leicestershire
A company museum. Corsetry since 1856. Evolution of the Liberty Bodice. Evolution of the brassière from the Victorian camisole to the Edwardian bust bodice and through to the present day.
Opening times Awaiting display facilities.

Central Museum and Art Gallery, Guildhall Road, Northampton, Northamptonshire
Local shoemaking industry. Footwear collections.
Opening times M, Tu., W, F 10–6; Th., Sa. 10–8.

C. & J. Clark's Shoe Museum, Street, Somerset
A company museum. History of shoemaking and of the company.
Opening times M–F 10–4.45; Sa. 10–1.

Coal

Science Museum, Buile Hill Park, Salford, Lancashire
    Buile Hill No. 1 Pit. Coalmining exhibits.
    Opening times M–Sa. 10–6 (Oct.–Mar. 10–5); Su. 2–5,
    April–Sept. Closed Good F, Christmas Day, Boxing Day,
    New Year's Day.

Edge-tool making

Abbeydale Industrial Hamlet, Abbeydale Road South, Sheffield,
South Yorkshire, S7 2QW
    Eighteenth-century scythe works, with Huntman-type
    crucible-steel furnace, tilt-hammers, grinding-shop and
    hand-forges.
    Opening times Weekdays 10–5; Su. 11–5. Spring Bank
    Holiday to Late Summer Bank Holiday, open until 8 daily.
Shepherd Wheel, Whiteley Wood, Sheffield, South Yorkshire
    Cutler's water-powered grinding-shop.
    Opening times   On application to the City Museum, Weston
    Park, Sheffield, S10 2TP.
Sticklepath Museum, Sticklepath, Okehampton, Devon EX20
2NW
    Nineteenth-century water-powered edge-tool works, restor-
    ed and with the equipment in working order. History of the
    works, the Finch Foundry. Gallery of water-power.
    Opening times   Daily 11–6.

Electrical engineering

Ferranti Ltd.'s Museum, Hollinwood, Lancashire
    A company museum. History of the company and of
    electrical engineering.
    Opening times   By appointment with the Company Archi-
    vist.

Fishing

Scottish Fisheries Museum, St. Ayles, Harbourhead, Anstruther,
Fife, KY10 3AB
    Fishing techniques. Ships' gear. Navigation equipment.
    Model fishing vessels. Aquarium.
    Opening times Apr.–Oct., M–Sa. 10–12.30, 2–6. Nov.–
    Mar., daily ex. Tu. 2.30–4.30.

Maritime Museum for East Anglia, Marine Parade, Great Yarmouth, Norfolk

Maritime history of the area. Fishing. North Sea oil and gas. Life-saving.

Opening times June–Sept., daily 10–1, 2–8. Oct.–May, M–F 10–1, 2–5.30.

Town Docks Museum, Queen Victoria Square, Kingston upon Hull, North Humberside

History of whaling. Maritime history of the city.

Opening times See locally.

Maritime Museum, aboard the lightship 'Guillemot', Wexford Harbour, Co. Wexford, Eire

Maritime history of Wexford. Nineteenth-century logbooks of Wexford schooners. Documents relating to vessels trading between Wexford and New Brunswick. Ships' models.

Opening times Daily 10.30–9.

Food and drink industries

Guinness Museum, Arthur Guinness and Co. Ltd., St. James's Gate, Dublin, Eire

Company museum. History of the company and of brewing in Ireland. Brewing equipment. Cooper's tools. Transport used in the industry. Advertising.

Opening times Sept.–May, M–F 11–12.45, 2–4.15. June–Aug., M–F 11–4.15.

Tate and Lyle Museum, Love Lane Refinery, Liverpool, Merseyside

Company museum. Sugar-refining equipment and processes.

Opening times 9–5, on application.

R. White and Son's Museum, Albany Road, London SE5

Company museum. Mineral water manufacturing and bottles.

Opening times By appointment.

The Carrow Museum, Carrow Abbey, Colman Foods Limited, Carrow, Norwich, NOR 75A, Norfolk

Company museum. Development of the company and all its products – starch, laundry blue, baby foods, soft drinks, etc.

Opening times By special arrangement only with the Internal Information Officer (0603–60166).

The Mustard Museum, The Mustard Shop, 3 Bridewell Alley,
Norwich, Norfolk, NR2 1AQ

The shop was opened for the celebrations of the 150th
anniversary of the partnership between Jeremiah and James
Colman (1823), and is fashioned in the style of the late
nineteenth century. Implements used in mustard-making.
Advertising material, packaging. Photographs illustrating
the development of the company and the family.

Opening times Daily ex. Th. and Su. 9–5.30.

Mill Museum, Shop Street, Tuam, Co. Galway, Eire

300-year-old cornmill, with exhibits illustrating milling
techniques and processes.

Opening times M–Sa. 10.30–12.30, 3–6; Su. 3–6.

Furniture-making

Wycombe Chair and Local History Museum, Castle Hill House,
Priory Avenue, High Wycombe, Buckinghamshire

Chairs, especially the Windsor chair. Tools and equipment
for chairmaking.

Opening times M, Tu., Th., F, Sa. 10–1, 2–5. Closed W,
Su. and Bank Holidays.

Glass-making

Pilkington Glass Museum, Pilkington Bros. Ltd., Prescot Road,
St. Helens, Merseyside, WA10 3TT

History of glass-making techniques, and of the company.

Opening times M–F 10–5 (Mar.–Oct. W 10–9); Sa., Su
and Bank Holidays 2–4.30.

Locks

Union Works Museum, Gower Street, Willenhall, West Midlands,
WV13 1JX

Company museum. History of locks and of the company.

Opening times By appointment.

Mechanical engineering

Avery Historical Museum, Soho Foundry, Birmingham 40, West
Midlands

Company museum. Machines and equipment illustrating
the history of weighing.

Opening times During factory hours, by appointment.

British Typewriter Museum, 137 Stewart Road, Bournemouth, Dorset
Collection illustrating a century of typewriter production.
Opening times M–Sa. 9-1, 2–5.30.

R. A. Lister Museum, Dursley, Gloucestershire, GL11 4HS
Company museum. Agricultural machinery and other products of the company since 1867.
Opening times By appointment (0453–4141).

Monks Hall Museum, 42 Wellington Road, Eccles, Lancashire, M30 0NP
Nasmyth machinery, including steam hammer. Steam engines.
Opening times M–F 10–6; Sa. 10–5.

Stradbally Steam Museum, Stradbally, Co. Leix, Eire
Steam engines and steam engine models. Many of the full-sized items are of Irish manufacture. Early steam-powered farm implements. Steam rollers.
Opening times May–Sept. 2–8. Oct.–Apr. 2–5.

Metals

Morwellham Quay, Morwellham, near Tavistock, Devon, PL19 8JL
Museum based on nineteenth century copper port, illustrating the history and techniques of the local copper industry.
Opening times Apr.–Sept. 10–6. Oct.–Mar. 10–dusk.

Tolgus Tin, Portreath Road, Redruth, Cornwall
Working Cornish tin-streams, with restored machinery and equipment, including stamps, round frames, rag frames and dipper wheels.
Opening times M–F 10–5.30. May–Sept. also Su. 10–5.30. Closed Good F and Christmas week.

Mining, quarrying (other than coal)

Llechwedd Slate Caverns, Blaenau Ffestiniog, Gwynedd
Nineteenth-century slate mine. Tableaux of miners and their equipment. Operating miners' tramway. Demonstrations and displays illustrating the production of roofing slates.
Opening times Daily, including Bank Holidays 10–5.15.

North Wales Quarrying Museum, Llanberis, Gwynedd, LL55 4TY

In the former workshops of Dinorwic Slate Quarries Company. History and techniques of slate-quarrying and processing at Dinorwic.

Opening times May–Sept., daily 9.30–7.

Wheal Martyn Museum of the China Clay Industry, Wheal Martyn, Carthew, St. Austell, Cornwall

History of the extraction and processing of china clay, based on a partially restored clay works (1880).

Opening times Apr.–Oct., daily 10–6.

Pencils

Pencil Museum, Cumberland Pencil Co. Ltd., Greta Bridge, Keswick, Cumbria

Company museum. History of pencil-making from 1558 to the present day.

Opening times May–Sept., M–F 9–12.30, 1.30–5.30.

Photography, film-making

Kodak Museum, Wealdstone, Harrow, Middlesex

History of photography and cinematography.

Opening times M–F 9–12, 1.30–4.30, by appointment.

Fox Talbot Museum, Lacock Abbey, Lacock, near Chippenham, Wiltshire

Life and achievements of William Henry Fox Talbot (1800–77) inventor of photography.

Opening times Feb.–Oct., daily 11–6.

Barnes Museum of Cinematography, Fore Street, St. Ives, Cornwall

History of cinematography and photographic processes.

Opening times Apr.–Sept., M–Sa. 11–5.

Pottery, porcelain

The Wedgwood Museum, Josiah Wedgwood and Sons Ltd., Barlaston, Stoke-on-Trent, Staffordshire, ST12 9ES

A company museum. Early Wedgwood ware and the techniques of its manufacture.

Opening times M–F 9–5 by appointment only (tel: Barlaston 2141).

City Museum and Art Gallery, Broad Street, Hanley, Stafford-shire

Staffordshire pottery and porcelain, and the methods by which it has been made.

Opening times M–Sa. 10–6; Su. 2.30–5.

William Cookworthy Museum, Old Grammar School, 108 Fore Street, Kingsbridge, Devon

Life and achievements of Cookworthy (1705–80) discoverer of china clay in Cornwall and of the method of making true porcelain from it.

Opening times M–Sa. 11–6.

Cheddleton Flint Mill, near Leek, Staffordshire

Water-driven mill used to grind calcined flints for use in china-manufacturing.

Opening times Apr.–Oct., Sa., Su. 2–5.

Gladstone Pottery Museum, Uttoxeter Road, Longton, Stoke-on-Trent, ST3 1PQ

A Victorian 'Potbank', conserved as a working museum. Four bottle ovens. Engine house and sliphouse restored to working order. A variety of pottery is produced using traditional methods. History of the Staffordshire potteries. Tile collection. Working tools and machinery.

Opening times Tu.–Sa. 10.30–5.30; Su. 2–6. Closed M.

Spode-Copeland Museum and Art Gallery, Church Street, Stoke-on-Trent, Staffordshire

Collections of early Spode blue-printed ware, bone china and stone china, and the wares of Copeland and Garrett.

Opening times M–F 10–4, by appointment only.

The Dyson Perrins Museum of Worcester Porcelain, The Royal Porcelain Works, Severn Street, Worcester, Worcestershire

The Royal Porcelain Works and its products.

Opening times M–F 9–12.30, 2–4. May–Sept. also Sa. 9–12.30, 2–4.

Textiles

Lewis Museum of Textile Machinery, Blackburn, Lancashire

Technical development of the spinning and weaving industries. Demonstrations.

Opening times M–F 9.30–8; Sa. 9.30–6.

Tonge Moor Textile Machinery Museum, Tonge Moor Road, Bolton, Lancashire

Historic textile machines, including Crompton's mule,

Hargreaves' jenny and Arkwright's water-frame.

Opening times M, Tu., Th., F 9.30–7.30; W 9.30–1; Sa. 9.30–5.30. Closed Bank Holidays.

Wellbrook Beetling Mill, Cookstown, Co. Tyrone, Northern Ireland

Eighteenth-century water-powered fulling mill, with nineteenth-century modifications.

Opening times Apr.–Sept., W–M 2–6.

Newtown Woollen Industry Museum, Commercial Street, Newtown, Powys

History of Newtown as a woollen centre. Techniques of wool processing and woollen manufacturing.

Opening times Apr.–Sept., Tu.–Sa. 2–4.30.

Water-supply

Bristol Waterworks Company Museum, P.O. Box 218, Bridgwater Road, Bristol, Avon, BS99 7AU

Waterworks equipment. Two beam engines preserved at Blagdon Pumping Station.

Opening times By written appointment only.

Springhead Pumping Station Museum, Yorkshire Water Authority (Eastern Division), Kingston-upon-Hull, North Humberside, HU10 6RA

Waterworks equipment, including Cornish beam engine.

Opening times By appointment: apply to the Water Authority, Alfred Gelder Street, Kingston-upon-Hull, HU1 2HE.

Ryhope Pumping Station and Museum, Ryhope, Sunderland, Tyne and Wear, SR2 0ND

In pumping station (1868), with two beam engines. History of pumping and water-supply.

Opening times Easter–Sept., Sa. and Bank Holidays 10–6; Su. 2–6. Other times by appointment (tel: Sunderland 210235).

Coleham Pumping Station, Longden Coleham, Shrewsbury, Shropshire

Contains two beam engines (1900).

Opening times W, F 2–5.

Wine

Harvey's Wine Museum, 12 Denmark Street, Bristol, Avon, BS99 7JE

Company museum. History of the Bristol wine trade.
Opening times By appointment only. M–F 2.30 and 6.30, conducted tours.

Libraries and archives

For most people interested in industrial archaeology who want to find out more about a particular site or building, or fit it into the wider context of an industry or the development of a district, one of the major regional libraries, such as Birmingham, Manchester or Plymouth, will provide all the facilities one can reasonably require. A journey to London will be necessary only when, as in the case of the British Transport records or those of the Coal Board, the archive is a national one. The Public Record Office and the British Museum Library are to be avoided whenever possible. They are always exceedingly crowded, seats are difficult to find, and the service of books and documents gets worse each year. One can usually do as well or better elsewhere, and without the formality of obtaining a reader's ticket.

Anyone, except the verminous, drunk, incontinent, noisy and aggressive, can work in a public library or public record office as a matter of right. For university libraries one has to obtain special permission, but this is rarely refused, if the reason for needing to use the library is clearly stated and if there is good reason to believe that the books or documents cannot be conveniently consulted elsewhere. The nationalised industries normally give good facilities to people who can produce evidence that they are serious students, but private companies are likely to be much more difficult, partly for real or imagined reasons of commercial security and partly because, understandably, they are simply unwilling to bother to have strangers about the place.

The golden rule when looking for information or carrying out research is to go first to the places where there is no problem of entry and to consider other sources only if and when one has reached a dead end.

The search for material can be made much quicker and easier by using the published reference works to the main types of collection. These are:

Libraries and Museums

The Libraries, Museums and Art Galleries Year Book gives all public and special libraries, museums and art galleries in the British Isles, with an indication of their scope and of any special collections they may have.

The *ASLIB Directory* (Association of Special Libraries) lists and describes in some detail all the specialised libraries in Great Britain.

Information about public libraries alone can be found in a Library Association publication, *Libraries in the United Kingdom and the Republic of Ireland.*

Public Records

The Public Record Office (Chancery Lane, London) issued a *Guide to the Public Record Office* in 1963. A *Supplement* to it appeared in 1968. The Public Record Office acts as a repository for the records of most Government departments, which are transferred to it regularly. The Scottish Record Office in Edinburgh and the Public Record Office of Northern Ireland in Belfast fulfil the same function for records relating to these countries. Parliament, however, and a few Government departments retain all or some of their records separately.

The publications of these three Record Offices are listed in *Government Publications, Sectional List 24: British National Archives*, which is published by HMSO and can be found in all major libraries.

Records of local authorities are sometimes deposited in a local library or record office, where they can be easily consulted, and sometimes remain in the custody of the authority itself, in which case a formal application to see them has to be made to the Clerk to the authority. A full list of all officially recognised record repositories is given in the booklet, *Record Repositories in Great Britain*, published in 1973 by HMSO. It is a useful asset to buy and keep. This, unfortunately, was compiled before the local authority boundary changes and consequently needs a certain amount of interpretation. A check with the latest edition of *The Municipal Year Book* or *The Local Government Manual and Directory* will make sure that the name and territory of each new authority in England and Wales is up-to-date. Information about local authorities in Scotland is to be found in *The County and Municipal Year*

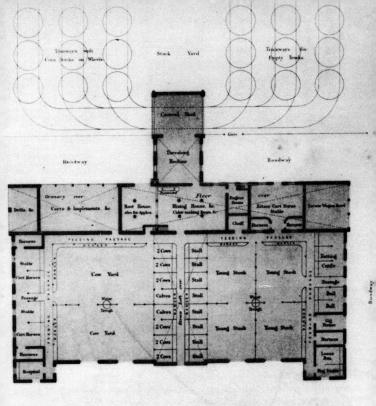

Plan of new farm buildings constructed in 1850 for Lord
Balem at Uphampton, in Herefordshire. Now in the Museum
of English Rural Life, Reading.

*Farming, as the National Farmers' Union has been reminding
us for thirty years and more, is an industry and the industrial
archaeologist does well not to neglect it. Farm buildings, such
as these at Uphampton, were, in every sense of the word,
factories. Built more or less regardless of expense in the golden
days of Victorian high-farming, they embodied the latest
technical ideas and housed the most up-to-date and labour-
saving machinery, often with a steam engine to drive it. Maps
such as this one often showed which machinery was located
where, information which is only rarely available to us in the
case of conventional factory buildings.*

Book for Scotland. The Municipal Year Book contains information about local authorities in Northern Ireland.

Many record repositories issue their own lists of contents and accessions.

Private Records

A large number of personal, family and business archives have been placed in public repositories, where they can usually be consulted without difficulty. The transfer of such archives is taking place all the time and it is not easy to keep up-to-date with what is where. The Royal Commission on Historical Manuscripts, which incorporates the National Register of Archives, has published since 1957 an annual *List of Accessions to Repositories*, setting out the new acquisitions of libraries and record repositories throughout the country, and the Business Archives Council and the Business Archives Council for Scotland can often help with advice and suggestions about the location and availability of commercial and industrial records.

The facilities for photography and photocopying vary enormously from one library and record office to another. As a general rule, the larger national institutions are infuriatingly slow and the smaller and local places much prompter and more satisfactory. The worst service is unquestionably that provided by the British Museum, where photocopying normally takes a week or more and photography not infrequently several months. At the other end of the scale, some local libraries and archives will carry out photocopying immediately and others the next day. The quality is sometimes not what one might wish, but the copy will always be legible and the prodigious saving of time, by comparison with hand-copying, makes even the highest-priced photocopying very cheap.

It is worth remembering, incidentally, that, for some extraordinary reason, photocopying carries no VAT if one does it oneself, which is often permitted, or encouraged, but full VAT if a member of the library staff takes it in hand.

Section Five

Organisations and institutions likely to be helpful

Until it came to a much-regretted end in 1974, the *Journal of Industrial Archaeology* had the useful habit of publishing a list of local industrial archaeology societies in November each year. The list was, of course, entirely factual and gave no more than the name of the society and the name and address of the secretary. No attempt was made to indicate which societies were enterprising and thriving and which were moribund. All, on paper, were of equal merit.

Since 1974, no reasonably up-to-date list has appeared and what follows is an attempt to fill the gap and, at the same time, to give a certain amount of tactful, but, one hopes, helpful information about each society, on the basis of personal contacts. It needs to be said at the outset, and as plainly as possible, that no two people who join a society, whether for industrial archaeology or for any other purpose, are looking for precisely the same thing, and that, for this reason, recommending a society is almost as difficult and thankless a task as recommending a restaurant. And, like restaurants, societies rise and fall very fast, according to the ability of the management.

Having made this point, one probably does best to begin with a very good society indeed, which happens to be in the capital, London. The Greater London Industrial Archaeology Society, generally known as GLIAS, covers a huge area and it needs to have a first-class organisation in order to survive, let alone prosper. After several years of experiment, it has developed a framework of four secretaries, each with a different function, and eleven Borough Correspondents.

The General Enquiries Secretary, who also deals with items for the Society's quarterly *Newsletter*, is:

Adrian Tayler
28 Tower Hamlets Road
LONDON E17

The Membership Secretary is:

Vere Glass
69 St. Peter's Road
CROYDON
Surrey CRO 1HS

and there are also Secretaries for Events and for the Recording Group. The Borough Correspondents are responsible for Bexley, Bromley, Croydon, Greenwich, Harrow, Kingston, Lambeth and Southwark, Lewisham, Sutton, Waltham Forest and Westminster. New members, of whom there are about a hundred a year, are put in touch with their nearest Borough Correspondent and all members receive, with remarkable promptness, a six- or eight-page *Newsletter*.

The *Newsletter* contains an Editorial, a detailed Diary of Events, Reports on already accomplished events and a wide variety of News Items. 'Our events programme', says the Society, 'has a threefold aim – to give members a chance to visit sites of IA interest not normally accessible, to help get to know each other better by meeting both on visits and informally and, most important – and very enjoyable – to actually record sites before the inevitable (and often necessary) march of progress removes once and for all the evidence of a step in our historical development.'

A typical month's programme, from mid-March to mid-April 1975, shows how this works out in practice, and how the various events are well spread over the period. Abbreviated, the items are:

Saturday, March 15
    All-day recording session of 1836–60 warehouses in Montague Close. A training exercise.
Tuesday, March 18
    Evening Workshop at Goldsmith's College, to discuss four projects.
Wednesday, March 19
    Evening visit to the *Daily Express*.
Saturday, March 22
    Camden Transport Survey. All-day work in St Pancras–King's Cross area.
Tuesday, March 25
    Talk at Croydon Technical College. *Croydon's Firsts in Industrial Archaeology*.

Croydon Airport, 1928.

At this date, Croydon was the grandest and most up-to-date airport in the world, and photographs like this help one to recapture something of the privileged splendour of travelling by air in the pre-war years. The surviving archaeology, the former terminal building, nowadays has a forlorn and abandoned appearance, but it is interesting and important, not only for its elegant design and good workmanship, but for its size and scale. This tiny building, one has to remind oneself, was the hub of the prestigious Imperial Airways system and the passengers at the entrance had been transported by the Company from London in one of the most comfortable and expensive vehicles available.

Thursday, April 3

Talk at Croydon Technical College. *Henry Overton and the Croydon Gas Co.*

Tuesday, April 8

Pub lunch at Fleet Street. 'A lunch get-together for members working within reach of Ludgate Circus'.

Saturday, April 12

Mortlake Peramble. An afternoon guided walk around the Mortlake–Barnes area.

Monday, April 14

Lunch in Goodge Street, W.1, 'to meet fellow-members working in the area'.

Friday, April 18

Coffee evening in Twickenham, at the home of two members doing work on Thames barges, on Brentford and on street furniture.

It is easy for those living in the provinces to say that anything is possible in London, because the opportunities are so much greater, but Londoners can easily retaliate that everything else – publicity, recruitment, organisation – is more difficult in London, because of the sheer size of the city. But the main point is that GLIAS has discovered a recipe that works, which pleases a wide range of people and which makes a mass of useful research possible. The GLIAS programme gives people new to industrial archaeology an idea of the kind of help and encouragement which a really good, well-run society can provide.

Spreading outwards over the South-East from London, these groups are available:

The Faversham Society

Secretary: Arthur Percival, 42 Newton Road, Faversham, Kent, ME13 8PU

This is probably the best local history society in Britain, covering all branches of local history and with a special interest in the Faversham Gunpowder Works, which it has helped to preserve. It also keeps a close and constructive eye on environmental problems and tries to spot developers' misdeeds before they happen.

Members of the Faversham Society carrying out restoration work on part of the former Gunpowder Works.

Once an industrial site is abandoned, it takes only a few years before the weather, vandals, thieves and the growth of vegetation turn it into a ruin. Clearing it, excavating it and restoring it is a slow task, requiring a great deal of patience and hard work, as well as knowledge and imagination. But, as the Faversham Society has shown, enthusiasm is what counts most and much of the skill required can be learnt on the job.

Kingston Polytechnic Industrial Archaeology Society
Secretary: Bryan Woodriff, Kingston Polytechnic, Penrhyn Road, Kingston-upon-Thames, Surrey

A staff-student society, which in the course of its researches asks for, and gets, the co-operation of many members of the general public in the Kingston area.

Maidstone Area Industrial Archaeology Group
Secretary: R. J. Spain, 'Trevarno', Roseacre Lane, Bearsted, Maidstone, Kent

A small group, interested in a wide range of Medway industries.

Rickmansworth Historical Society
Secretary: E. V. Parrott, 66 The Queens Drive, Rickmansworth, Hertfordshire

A local history society, a number of whose members carry out investigations into the industrial history of the Rickmansworth area, especially paper-making.

Surrey Archaeological Society: Industrial Archaeology Group
Secretary: D. J. Turner, Castle Arch, Guildford, Surrey

Within the society, there is a loosely-knit group of people whose interests lie mainly within the field of industry and transport.

Watford and District Industrial History Society
Secretary: R. Beattie, 23 St. Lawrence Way, Bricket Wood, Watford, Hertfordshire

Watford has been an important industrial centre for more than a century, with brewing, printing, paper and railways as major activities. The society is trying to gather information about them at a time when the older industries are fading away rapidly and being replaced by new sources of employment.

The Eastern counties, for some unexplained reason, are not well covered. The large area which includes Essex, Cambridgeshire, Suffolk, Norfolk and Lincolnshire is represented by only three societies. They are:

Cambridge Society for Industrial Archaeology

Secretary: N. A. Smith, 4 Springfield Road, Cambridge, CB4 1AD

This well-established society, which includes both University and non-University members, carries out work over a much wider area of Cambridgeshire than its name suggests.

Norfolk Industrial Archaeology Society

Secretary: Mrs. J. Mackie, 2 Mill Corner, Hingham, Norwich, Norfolk, NOR 23X

This much-needed society, which draws its strength mainly from the Norwich area itself, has many years of work ahead of it, recording the evidence of the county's agriculture and sea-based industries, which have been neglected by both conservationists and industrial archaeologists for far too long.

Society for Lincolnshire History and Archaeology: Industrial Archaeology Sub-Committee

Secretary: Mrs. C. M. Wilson, Museum of Lincolnshire Life, Burton Road, Lincoln

The Lincolnshire Society, based at the excellent County Museum, has a group with specialised industrial archaeology interests closely linked to it and sharing the Museum's general facilities.

The North-East, with its strong industrial traditions, has a number of thriving societies. Including those in Yorkshire, they are:

Batley Museum Society, Industrial Archaeology Section

Secretary: Mrs. J. M. Ashworth, 16 High Cote, Riddlesden, Keighley, Yorkshire

A small group, with a programme ranging from fieldwork to lectures and a spectrum of interests which shades off from folk-lore through handicrafts to manufacturing industry.

Bradford Archaeology Group: Industrial Archaeology Section

Secretary: Stuart W. Feather, Bradford City Art Gallery and Museum, Moorside Mills, Moorside Road, Bradford, BD2 3HP

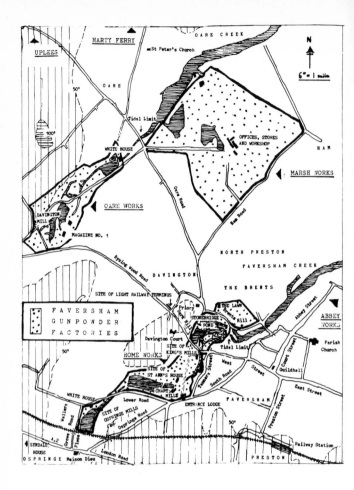

Sketch-map of the area covered by the gunpowder factories at Faversham, Kent.

This map illustrates the work of the Faversham Society quite as much as it does the extent of the once-important local gunpowder works. Without the organised efforts of this exceptionally vigorous society, the map and the investigation of the sites on it would have been impossible. The Faversham Society, however, is concerned with the history and well-being of the district as a whole, not merely with its industrial archaeology. It puts industrial archaeology, one might say, into its proper, meaningful, human context.

This is another society-within-a-society, with a museum base. It is not, as sometimes happens, overshadowed by the parent society and has a life of its own. Anyone contemplating joining it can rest assured that he need have nothing to do with prehistoric archaeologists and medievalists unless he wants to.

University of Bradford, Industrial Archaeology Unit
Secretary: Dr. John Diaper, The University, Richmond Road, Bradford, BD7 1DP
A self-contained University group, drawing its members from different departments of the University.

Durham Industrial Archaeology Group
Secretary: D. Wilcock, 26 Bede Terrace, Bowburn, Durham, DH6 5DT
Some confusion may be caused by the fact that Mr. Wilcock is the Secretary of both the Durham and the North-Eastern Group. These are two quite distinct organisations, one dealing with the opportunities of Durham and its immediate area and the other with a responsibility for the whole of the North-East. One can belong to either or to both, according to the amount of time and energy at one's disposal.

Durham University Group for Industrial Archaeology
Secretary: Christopher Hinde, Dunelm House, New Elvet, Durham
Another purely University group, so far as its membership is concerned, but one which, by choice and necessity, maintains close links with local industries and people.

East Riding Agricultural Machinery Preservation Society
Secretary: H. E. Kirk, Louvain, Rowley Road, Little Weighton, Kingston-upon-Hull
This is essentially a band of specialists, actively interested in the preservation of tractors and all types of farm machinery and equipment.

Huddersfield Industrial Archaeology Society
Secretary: Robert Whitehead, 119 Coniston Avenue, Dalton, Huddersfield, Yorkshire
An active and rather serious-minded society, not given to the lunch and coffee-evening type of programme.

North-East Industrial Archaeology Society
Secretary: D. Wilcock, 26 Bede Terrace, Bowburn, Durham, DH6 5DT

The major society for the North-East, closely linked to the Museum for the North-East, at Beamish. It does excellent work as a co-ordinating body and as an information centre, but also runs its own programme.

Northern Cavern and Mine Research Society
Secretary: K. Walls, 33 Gledhow Avenue, Roundhay, Leeds 8

For the active and adventurous only.

Sunderland Industrial Archaeology Group
Secretary: George Edwards, 3 Broxbourne Terrace, Sunderland, Tyne and Wear

This group is particularly interested in shipping and in the heavy industries for which the area is renowned, but welcomes members whose interests take them in other directions.

Teesside Industrial Archaeology Group
Secretary: David M. Tomlin, 8 Loweswater Crescent, Stockton-on-Tees, Teesside, TS18 4PY

A general-interest group.

Tyne Industrial Archaeology Group
Secretary: R. M. Higgins, Waterhouse & Partners, Park View House, Front Street, Newcastle-upon-Tyne, NE7 7TZ

The Teesside and Tyne Groups are of considerable local importance. Each concentrates on fieldwork within a fairly compact area and there is no shortage of material for anyone willing to search for it.

Yorkshire Archaeological Society: Industrial History Section
Secretary: Mrs. N. M. Cooper, 307 Spen Lane, Leeds, LS16 5BD

This Section, as its name suggests, is concerned with the broad field of industrial history, rather than with the somewhat narrower one of industrial archaeology, although the archaeological aspect of it is by no means unimportant. Anyone whose interests tend towards local history or oral history would find this a particularly rewarding society to join.

North of the Border, the Scottish Society for Industrial Archaeology has established itself as very much the national society, with members widely scattered over the country. There is a high concentration in the Glasgow area and around the Clyde, where the bulk of the membership is almost certainly found. This is a consequence partly of the size and industrial importance of Glasgow and partly of the pioneering work carried out by Dr. John Butt and his colleagues in the Department of Economic History in the University of Strathclyde, which for the past ten years has been the centre of industrial archaeology in Scotland, and the base from which *Industrial Archaeology* was edited during the last five years of that journal's existence.

The three Scottish societies are:

Abertay Historical Society: Industrial Archaeology Section
Secretary: D. Bruce Walker, 149 Strathern Road, West Ferry, Dundee, DD5 1BR

Clackmannanshire Field Studies Society: Industrial Archaeology Section
Secretary: Mrs. E. K. Kennedy, 26 Victoria Street, Alloa, Clackmannanshire

Scottish Society for Industrial Archaeology
Secretary: D. M. Dickie, Teachers' Centre, Branshill Road, Alloa, Clackmannanshire

The North-West has a convenient scatter of societies, and nobody in this part of Britain is likely to find himself at any great distance from one. Somewhat inevitably, the major points of strength are in the Manchester and Liverpool areas, and there are unfortunate gaps in the Oldham and Bolton areas of Lancashire and, very surprisingly, in Crewe, where the old railway culture has not yet spawned a society to study it and its heirs.

Chester and District Industrial Archaeology Society
Secretary: G. R. Coppack, Sunnycot, 1 Ash Grove, Little Sutton, Wirral, Cheshire L66 1PP

A mixed membership of people who work in the Wirral and

those who merely live there and commute, with a useful cross-fertilisation of ideas and energy between the two.

Cumberland and Westmorland Antiquarian and Archaeological Society: Industrial Archaeology Committee

Joint Secretaries: M. Davies-Shiel, Lilac Cottage, Lake Road, Bowness-on-Windermere, and Dr. J. D. Marshall, Department of History, University of Lancaster, Bailrigg, Lancaster

An influential body, headed by the authors of the standard book on the industrial archaeology of the region.

Isle of Man Natural History and Antiquarian Society, Field Section, Industrial Archaeology Group

Secretary: L. Quilliam, c/o Manx Museum, Douglas, Isle of Man

The cumbersome title of this group conceals ten years of wide-ranging activity in what might not appear at the outset to be a very promising field. Members of the group have been investigating hotels and the tourist industry, lead and zinc mining, tramways, breweries, shipping, fishing and other Isle of Man specialities.

Manchester Region Industrial Archaeology Society

Secretary: Dr. R. L. Hills, c/o Manchester Museum of Science and Technology, 97 Grosvenor Street, Manchester, M1 7HF

This society was founded by a group of academics fired with intense patriotism for local industries and determined to create a museum worthy of them. It, like the Museum, has drawn much strength from the support given by the University, but it is in no sense a University society and would-be members who are not academics have no reason to be frightened off.

Northern Mill Engine Society

Secretary: Trevor Lees, 2 Brocklebank Road, Rochdale, Lancashire

A society of hard-working aficionados, drawn from all walks of life and with only one passion, to acquire and restore steam engines from cotton and woollen mills, in order to save these beautiful objects from destruction and to preserve them for posterity.

North-Western Society for Industrial Archaeology and History

Secretary: Mrs. P. Paget-Tomlinson, City of Liverpool Museum, William Brown Street, Liverpool, L3 8EN

This is the North-West's major industrial archaeology society, based in a museum which itself has a very fine section devoted to the history of industry and technology. Each year this pleasantly democratic society organises a well-mixed programme of lectures, guided walks and field projects, and it has something with which not all organisations of this kind are blessed, an efficient administration.

Rochdale Society for the Study of the History of Industry and Technology

Secretary: D. Ternent, 298 Hatfield, Ashfield Valley, Rochdale, Lancashire

A well-located society, with special strengths in cotton and engineering and with a membership that is agreeably spread socially, in the traditional cotton-district fashion.

The main difficulty about the Midlands is that no-one is sure where they begin or end, so that a Midlands Society for Industrial Archaeology would have little appeal or cohesion. Birmingham, Leicester and Stafford have no particular wish to know one another. However, if one may dare to define the area, the Midlands societies are:

Birmingham and Warwickshire Archaeological Society: Industrial Archaeology Research Group

Secretary: Dr. Jennifer Tann, Department of Industrial Administration, University of Aston in Birmingham, Maple House, 158 Corporation Street, Birmingham 4

Dr. Tann is one of the most respected figures working in the field of industrial history. Her strong personal interest in industrial housing has communicated itself to the group, but its research activities are by no means confined to matters of housing.

Derbyshire Archaeological Society: Industrial Archaeology Section

Secretary: L. J. Stead, 48a Sandbed Lane, Belper, Derby

Textiles, engineering, quarrying and railways are the society's principal interests, but many other industries have been carried on in Derbyshire and the Secretary would be equally pleased to hear from people whose tastes do not come under these headings.

Leicestershire Industrial History Society
Secretary: R. N. Thomson, 'Three Gables', Queen Street, Markfield, Leicester

The society's energies are devoted to the study of industrial history as a whole and not merely to industrial archaeology, but industrial archaeologists are not treated as a lesser or a comic breed and may well find the company of industrial historians refreshing and stimulating.

Northamptonshire Industrial Archaeology Group
Secretary: G. H. Starmer, 17 Mayfield Road, Northampton, NN3 2RE

'Group' implies something smaller than a society, and this is certainly not a large society, although it has no shortage of useful things to do and is very willing to expand.

Peak District Mines Historical Society
Secretary: P. J. Naylor, 85 Peveril Road, Beeston, Nottingham

An old-established society, containing a high proportion of members energetic enough to carry out underground exploration. This is not a library-based or lecture-loving group.

Redditch Industrial Archaeology Society
Secretary: C. A. Beardsmore, 127 Beaumont Road, Bournville, Birmingham

Redditch is the traditional centre of needle-making in the Midlands, although the local industries are now much more varied. The society has done a great deal to investigate the history and relics of needle-making and other trades of the Birmingham area, at a time when extensive redevelopment has made such work urgent.

Staffordshire Industrial Archaeology Society
Secretary: F. Brook, 15 Widecombe Avenue, Weeping Cross, Stafford

The secretary of this society is one of the pillars of the industrial archaeology movement in Britain. He is greatly helped by the rapidly-changing nature of Staffordshire's industries, which brings a constant supply of new, young, intelligent and potentially active people into the area.

Wolverhampton Polytechnic: Study Centre for Industrial Archaeology and Business History of the West Midlands

Secretary: W. A. Smith, The Polytechnic, Wolverhampton, West Midlands

This is primarily a research centre, which publishes the results of its work in *West Midlands Studies*. A number of those connected with the Centre, however, are active in research projects within the West Midlands and rely on local people, both in groups and individually, to help them with fieldwork.

Wolverton and District Archaeological Society

Secretary: R. J. Ayers, 13 Vicarage Walk, Stony Stratford, Wolverton, Buckinghamshire

This is an unusual type of local society, which believes in the value of campaigning. Its village meetings, to arouse interest and unlock material of historic interest, have been very successful and much of what is collected in this way by members of the society is concerned with the industrial history of the area.

When one considers the size of what is here taken as the Southern area – Sussex, Berkshire, Hampshire, Wiltshire – one cannot say that it is as yet well served by industrial archaeology societies, especially since two of those listed below are more or less closed groups, with membership restricted to the staff and students of the institutions in question. There would certainly appear to be room for societies in Brighton, Chichester and Eastleigh, all of which have interesting industrial traditions.

Basingstoke Industrial Archaeology Group (WEA)

Chairman: P. P. Morris, 103 Maldive Road, Basingstoke, Hampshire

A group formed of members of a local WEA class in industrial archaeology. The class, which changes its membership somewhat from year to year, is concerned with carrying out research projects within the Basingstoke area of Hampshire.

Berkshire Archaeological Society: Industrial Archaeology Group

Secretary: J. Kenneth Major, 2 Eldon Road, Reading, Berkshire, RG1 4DH

Council for British Archaeology, Group 9: Industrial Archaeology Sub-Committee

Secretary: J. Kenneth Major, 2 Eldon Road, Reading, Berkshire, RG1 4DH

Mr. Major, one of our leading authorities on water, wind and animal-power, is a protagonist of the idea that industrial archaeologists should join the local archaeology society and work from within it. He believes, like a number of other archaeologists, that such a course of action adds strength to the archaeological society and helps industrial archaeologists to maintain respectable standards of research and report-writing. As the above two entries show, he practises what he preaches.

Portsmouth Polytechnic: Industrial Archaeological Society

Secretary: Dr. R. C. Riley, Department of Geography, Portsmouth Polytechnic, Lion Terrace, Portsmouth, PO1 3HE

Like all university and college societies, the one at the Polytechnic has a more or less stable staff membership and a student membership which receives an annual blood transfusion.

Salisbury and South Wiltshire Industrial Archaeology Society

Secretary: Peter Goodhugh, 34 Countess Road, Amesbury, Salisbury, Wiltshire

It is curious that Swindon, the largest industrial centre in Wiltshire, has no industrial archaeology society, whereas the more rural southern part of the county benefits from a society which has been thriving for more than ten years.

Southampton University Industrial Archaeology Group

Secretary: J. B. Horne, Heathermount, Moor Hill, West End, Southampton, Hampshire

A student–staff group, closely linked to the University's Extra-Mural Department.

Sussex Industrial Archaeology Society

Secretary: A. J. Haselfoot, Albion House, Cobourg Place, Hastings, Sussex, TN34 3HY

This society covers, with remarkable success, the huge and unwieldy area of both East and West Sussex. It is closely associated with the University of Sussex and has an excellent record of publications.

Wiltshire Archaeological and Natural History Society: Industrial Archaeology Committee

Secretary: D. A. E. Cross, Wyndhams, Shrewton, Salisbury, Wiltshire

Wiltshire has an excellent County archaeological society, with its headquarters in Devizes. The Industrial Archaeology Committee's prime aim is to use the Society's facilities and organisation as a way of serving that part of the County which does not fall within the area of the Salisbury and South Wiltshire Society.

The South-Western counties are, on the whole, well provided with societies to meet the needs of industrial archaeologists and, equally important, all the societies are in a healthy condition. In this area – Avon, Somerset, Gloucestershire, Dorset, Devon, Cornwall – the opportunities are:

Bristol Industrial Archaeology Society (BIAS)

Secretary: Mrs. Joan Day, Hunter's Hill, Oakfield Road, Keynsham, Bristol, Avon, BS18 1JQ

This society's research work and publications probably reach the highest standard in Britain, under the influence of two universities, Bath and Bristol, and a good City Museum. There is an excellent programme of activities throughout the year.

Cornwall Archaeological Society: Industrial Archaeology Sub-Committee

Secretary: S. Beard, 6 Godolphin Way, Newquay, Cornwall

In the past, most of the historical side of Cornish industry has been looked after by the Cornish Engines Preservation Society and the Trevithick Society, both of which are national as much as local bodies. The Sub-Committee of the Archaeological Society helps to meet the requirements

of those whose all-consuming interest in industrial archaeology is not centred on steam engines and tin-mining.

Devon Industrial Archaeology Survey
Secretary: Michael Dower, Dartington Amenity Research Trust, Central Office, Skinner's Bridge, Dartington, Totnes, Devon

A Survey is not, properly speaking, a society, but the Devon Survey makes demands on the knowledge and skills of so many local people that it has taken on the function of a county-wide society.

The Devonshire Association: Industrial Archaeology Group
Secretary: R. M. L. Cook, 18 Margaret Park, Hartley Vale, Plymouth, Devon, PL3 5RR

The group is trying hard, and to a large extent with success, to prove that it does not share the élitist associations of the Devonshire Association, and to function as a democratising force within it. This is the kind of problem that is not well understood in Birmingham or South Lancashire.

A late nineteenth-century postcard of the Wheal Emma copper mine, near Gunnislake, Cornwall.

Our ancestors produced and sold postcards of what might nowadays be considered the most unlikely and unpromising subjects, and examples such as this of Wheal Emma constantly turn up, both loose and mounted in albums at sales and in junk shops. They are worth watching for, and to compare what is shown on the card with the ruined site which nowadays is all that is available for the industrial archaeologist to study makes a stimulating exercise in reconstruction.

The card by itself is not, of course, adequate background information, but it is a useful component. The more one knows about a site, the more the ruins mean.

Dorset Natural History and Archaeological Society: Industrial Archaeology Group

Secretary: D. Young, 20 Martel Close, Broadmayne, Dorchester, Dorset

This go-ahead county society was considerably involved in industrial history before industrial archaeology became a name. The Industrial Archaeology Group is a natural development of activities and interests which already existed, but the new name no doubt broadens the field of recruitment.

Exeter Industrial Archaeology Group

Secretary: Mrs. B. Entwistle, 5 Elm Grove Road, Topsham, Exeter, Devon, EX3 0EQ

This is a lecture-going-cum-fieldwork group with strong attachments to the Department of Economic History at the University.

Gloucestershire Society for Industrial Archaeology

Secretary: Miss A. Chatwin, 6 & 7 Montpellier Street, Cheltenham, Glos., GL50 1SX

The Gloucestershire Society, which is one of the oldest in Britain, has been fortunate in having had useful industrial connections from its earliest days. It is a markedly non-academic society and probably attracts a wide range of members for that reason.

Keynsham and Saltford Local History Society: Industrial Section

Secretary: R. Milner, 15 Chelmer Grove, Keynsham, nr. Bristol, Avon

The Keynsham and Saltford stretches of the River Avon were, during the eighteenth and much of the nineteenth centuries, the site of a number of industrial processes and local industrial archaeologists have a rich, if somewhat restricted field to plough.

Poole (WEA) Industrial Archaeology Group

Secretary: Alfred J. A. Cooksey, 18 Parkstone Avenue, Parkstone, Poole, Dorset, BH14 9LR

This group was founded in the early 1960s, as a development of WEA courses in industrial archaeology which were being run in the Poole area. It has continued, with something of a momentum of its own, ever since.

Somerset Industrial Archaeology Society

Chairman: Frank Hawtin, Quaking House, Milverton, Taunton, Somerset, TA4 1NG

The Somerset Archaeological Society is one of the county societies which has not thought fit to add a separate industrial archaeology section to itself, and the Industrial Archaeology Society was established to fill the gap, largely as a result of the energy and imagination of its present chairman, who, as Schools Museum Officer, had had much experience in organising surveys by young people on industrial archaeology sites.

Wales has so far shown less enthusiasm than any other part of Britain for setting up local societies for industrial archaeology. The indefatigable Douglas Hague, Inspector of Historic Monuments for Wales, is doing his best to remedy this, but with the whole of Wales as his parish and journeys frequently long and difficult, the task is a daunting one, and one can only appeal, on Mr. Hague's behalf, for all possible help.

Council for British Archaeology, Group 2: Industrial Archaeology Section

Secretary: Douglas B. Hague, Maesglas, Llanafan, Aberystwyth, Dyfed

South-East Wales Industrial Archaeology Society

Secretary: W. G. Hughes, 97 Wenallt Road, Rhiwbina, Cardiff, South Glamorgan

The general feeling in South Wales appears to be that industrial archaeology consists of coal, iron and docks and little else, and that since everything worth knowing about this holy trio is already known, what work could there be for a local group to do? The South-East Wales Society has had to achieve what successes it could in these not exactly encouraging circumstances.

South-West Wales Industrial Archaeology Society

Newsletter Editor: P. R. Reynolds, 12 Beaconsfield Way, Sketty, Swansea, West Glamorgan

The Irish, for many years, found it difficult to believe that they had any industrial archaeology at all. More recently, however, the truth has been revealed that Ireland, both north and south of the border, has a long history of industrial development and that both the Nine and the Five Counties are rich in industrial relics of all kinds.

Irish Society for Industrial Archaeology

Secretary: K. A. Mawhinney, 34 Lakelands Close, Blackrock, Co. Dublin

The Irish Society, which in practice covers only the Republic, has the formidable task of catching up with the backlog of recording and of educating both industry and the Government in the aims and possibilities of conservation.

By a strange irony, the South has a good industrial archaeology society and no national museum of science, industry or technology. The North, by contrast, has a first-class museum and no society.

It might be helpful, as a way of seeing the situation in its proper scale and perspective, to point out that, apart from London, the largest local or regional society has about 250 members and that most of the others have between 50 and 100. If one said that in all the societies put together there might be perhaps 6000 people and that of these possibly 4000 could reasonably be called active, it becomes clear that the field is as yet by no means overcrowded and that there is plenty of room for new recruits.

The subscription to local industrial archaeology societies ranges from £2 a year to £3. These figures are now too low to allow the societies to contact their members as frequently as they should and to publish a respectable bulletin and journal. They will certainly have to rise to £3–£4 if the work is to be done properly and the society is to stay in business.

Those who have come to regard Industrial Archaeology – the capitals become essential at this point – as a way of life, rather than a mere hobby, tend to belong to the:

Association for Industrial Archaeology
Church Hill, Ironbridge, Telford, Shropshire, TF8 7RE

and to attend its annual conference. These people are known as serious industrial archaeologists, to distinguish them from the different category who are in it merely for pleasure and personal education. Even more serious-minded people join the:

Newcomen Society for the Study of the History of Engineering and Technology
c/o The Science Museum, London SW7

which holds regular meetings to listen to learned papers, which are subsequently published in the Society's *Transactions*, and has a well-organised annual meeting, sometimes abroad. Members living in the centre part of England can enjoy the facilities of the:

Newcomen Society, Midlands Branch
Hon. Secretary: 147 Whirlowdale Road, Sheffield, Yorkshire

People who want to make contact with other local historians, rather than other industrial archaeologists or historians of technology, can usefully get in touch with:

The Standing Conference for Local History
26 Bedford Square, London WC1

This curiously named body is, in fact, the national clearing-house for all kinds of information about local history and local historians. It is responsible for a number of excellent, cheap publications which are aimed at the amateur historian and it maintains up-to-date details of local historical societies and their officers.

The Railway and Canal Historical Society
38 Station Road, Wylde Green, Sutton Coldfield, West Midlands

exercises a similar function within two specialised fields of transport.

The Inland Waterways Association
114 Regent's Park Road, London NW1

and

The Inland Waterways Protection Society
Grose-side, Cartledge Lane, Holmsfield, Sheffield

are concerned more with the effective use of Britain's waterways than with their history. The interests of two other bodies,

The Historic Aircraft Preservation Society
7 Baker Street, London W1

and

The Historic Commercial Vehicle Club
1 Pembury House, Abbey Park, Beckenham, Kent

are frankly nostalgic and antiquarian.

On the recording, as distinct from the information side, the following are the most important organisations:

National Record of Industrial Monuments
University of Bath, Claverton Down, Bath, Avon, BA2 7AY

This is a large card-index of technological sites and monuments, maintained on behalf of the Department of the Environment and the Council for British Archaeology. It depends for its success on completed cards being sent in by local groups and individuals and some areas have been much better than others about this.

National Monuments Record (which includes the National Building Record)
Fortress House, 23 Savile Row, London W1

This is the national picture archive for historic monuments. Twenty years ago it contained very little material of an industrial nature, but since then determined efforts have been made to put this right and the present position is much more satisfactory. Copies of the high-quality prints in the Record can be bought at a very reasonable price.

The various engineering organisations can often be very helpful in clearing up a problem connected with the past of their own profession, provided the question is clearly stated and that answering it does not involve a great deal of research and a typed letter several pages long. The principal bodies are:

Institute of Chemical Engineers
16 Belgrave Square, London SW1

Institute of Marine Engineers
Memorial Building, 76 Mark Lane, London EC3

Institute of Quarrying
62–64 Baker Street, London W1

Institute of Transport
80 Portland Place, London W1

Institution of Civil Engineers
Great George Street, London SW1

The Institution has a separate Panel for Historic Engineering Works, to which queries of an historical or archaeological nature should normally be addressed.

Institution of Electrical Engineers
Savoy Place, London WC2

Institution of Highway Engineers
14 Queen Anne's Gate, London SW1

Institution of Mechanical Engineers
1 Birdcage Walk, London SW1

Institution of Mining and Metallurgy
44 Portland Place, London W1

Institution of Mining Engineers
3 Grosvenor Crescent, London SW1

Institution of Structural Engineers
11 Upper Belgrave Street, London SW1

The Institution has a separate Historical Group, to which queries of an historical or archaeological nature should normally be addressed.

Institution of Water Engineers
6–8 Sackville Street, London W1

Iron and Steel Institute
4 Grosvenor Gardens, London SW1

Similar help can be obtained from the major industrial groups, such as:

The Brick Development Association
3 Bedford Row, London WC1
The Cement and Concrete Association
52 Grosvenor Gardens, London SW1
National Coal Board
Hobart House, Grosvenor Place, London SW1

When contact with the Government is required, the Department most likely to be useful is:

Department of the Environment
a Directorate of Ancient Monuments and Historic Buildings, 2 Marsham Street, London SW1
b Chief Inspector of Ancient Monuments and Historic Buildings, Fortress House, 23 Savile Row, London W1

For information of a national character concerning archives, the following are the best organisations to get in touch with, mainly as guides to the whereabouts of the material for which one is searching. An annual subscription to the first four will bring a regular flow of information about recent accessions and about special collections of documents.

British Record Society
Secretary: c/o Department of History, The University, Keele, Staffordshire

British Record Association
Secretary: c/o the Charterhouse, Charterhouse Square, London EC1

Business Archives Council
63 Queen Victoria Street, London EC4

National Register of Archives
Quality House, Quality Court, Chancery Lane, London WC2

British Transport Historical Records
66 Porchester Road, London W2

The catalogue of the National Film Archive is invaluable to anyone wishing to explore the past through the medium of old films. Membership of the British Film Institute, which shares the premises of the National Film Archive, brings considerable privileges and advantages, not only to people living in and near London. The address is:

National Film Archive
81 Dean Street, London W1

Another excellent source of films relating to rail and road transport is:

British Transport Films

Melbury House, Melbury Terrace, London NW1

And, spread over the whole panorama of nineteenth-century buildings, machines, people and ideas, is:

The Victorian Society

1 Priory Gardens, Bedford Park, London W4 1TT

Membership of this well-informed and influential body can do a great deal to put the industrial archaeologist's often rather over-specialised and parochial knowledge and interests into a broader, more sensible and more civilised context.

Getting one's bearings: the key inventions and technical developments

One needs a certain minimum of historical knowledge in order to understand the significance of what one is looking at. Historical illiterates, like other ignorant people, miss a lot, because they have nothing but their instincts and emotions to tell them if something is interesting or important or not. 'It's interesting because I like it' is a good beginning, but no more than a beginning. Interest feeds and grows on information. That is what information is for, or should be for. But there can be a lot of argument as to how large the 'certain minimum' of historical knowledge ought to be. Those with a vested interest in such matters – teachers and members of professional bodies, for instance – often give the impression, intentionally or unintentionally, of believing that nobody should be permitted to walk along a canal tow-path, visit an old pumping-station or take pictures of a Victorian housing estate without previously having attended courses in social and economic history, surveying, photography, and the development of technology, supported, naturally, by several years of wide and deep reading.

This attitude needs to be firmly and clearly labelled for what it is – rubbish. Life is much too short even to attempt to carry out in one's spare time all the things that the professionals quite properly achieve during their working hours and, in any case, the amateur is free and entitled to browse around until he finds some aspect of a subject which particularly interests him. Once this happens, he is extremely likely to want to find out all he possibly can about brickmaking, iron bridges, milling, glass bottles, or whatever his chosen speciality may turn out to be. The body of knowledge which individuals acquire in this way can be formidable. Experts in the history of industry and technology are certainly not only to be found on the staff of universities and museums.

But no-one is born an expert and without some kind of basic

framework of history one can flounder about for a long time. The list of key dates which follows says, in effect: 'This is a beginning, a set of bearings to guide you on your way, a pattern of events'. If it contains surprises, so much the better. It does no English person any harm to learn, for instance, that the great pioneers of the internal combustion engine were German or that the first public broadcasting station was in the United States. What is plain, however, even from a rapid reading of these pages, is the remarkable inventiveness and enterprise of the British up to about 1850 and the decline of their superiority after that time, as the Americans, Germans, and French especially, poured money, brains and determination into achieving technological progress.

It goes without saying, of course, that this is only one kind of list. Another would emphasise the social unrest and suffering caused by changes in industrial methods, another would be concerned with factory acts and the broad range of welfare legislation, another would be of the conventional political type, filled with details of wars, treaties and changes of government. The best list is the kind one constructs oneself, and, in a less expensive age it would have been pleasant and useful to have left sizable blank spaces, diary-like, after each item in our list, to give readers an opportunity to fill in their own digested pieces of information and key-points as they came across them. As things are, however, such desirable innovations have to await a kinder economic climate.

Aviation

1785 Blanchard and Jeffries cross the English Channel in a balloon
1804 Sir George Cayley constructs the first glider
1809 Cayley's paper, 'On Aerial Navigation', which laid the foundations of aerodynamics and flight control
1885 H. F. Phillips pioneers wind-tunnel experiments
1889 Otto Lilienthal invents the hang-glider, in Germany
1893 L. Hargrave invents the box-kite, in Australia
1900 Count von Zeppelin's first airship
1903 Orville and Wilbur Wright make first flight in a heavier-than-air machine, in the United States
1919 World's first scheduled flights, London–Paris

1920	Croydon becomes London's civil airport
1924	Imperial Airways established
1930	The first stewardesses, in the United States
1933-4	The first generation of modern-type aircraft – the Boeing 247, Douglas DC1 and Lockheed Electra – all-metal, low-wing monoplanes
1938	Boeing 314 Clipper flying-boat
1949	Boeing 377 Stratocruiser
1954	Boeing 707

Cement, concrete

1796	James Parker's patent for 'Roman cement'
1824	Joseph Aspdin's patent for 'a superior cement resembling Portland stone'
c.1838	'Concrete' first used in the modern sense – cement, aggregate and water thoroughly mixed before being placed in position
1845	The first reliable Portland cement made by I. C. Johnson, at Swanscomb, Kent
1854	W. B. Wilkinson's patent for reinforced concrete beams
1855	Jean Louis Lambot's patent for mesh-reinforced concrete
1857	Louis Cézanne invents the concrete mixer
1877	Thomas Russell Crampton patents his improved rotary kiln
1887	Installation of the first rotary cement-kiln, at Arlesey, Hertfordshire
1893	Ludwig Hatschar begins making asbestos-cement sheets, in Austria
1894	Augustus Sackett's American patent for plasterboard
1923	Corrugated asbestos-cement sheet first made in Britain
1926	Transit concrete-mixer first used in the United States
1927	Asbestos-cement pipes first made, at Widnes, Cheshire
1928	Pre-stressed concrete introduced in Germany by Fritz Dischinger

Chemicals

c.1690	Rock-salt discovered in Cheshire
1695	Nehemiah Grew's patent for making Epsom Salt, the first true patent medicine
1746	John Roebuck and Samuel Garbett pioneer, in Birmingham, the lead-chamber process for making sulphuric acid

1785   C. L. Berthollet discovers, in France, the bleaching action of chlorine

1789   Andrew Pears begins to make a transparent soap in Oxford Street, London

1791   Nicholas Leblanc develops, in France, a process for converting salt into soda

1799   Charles Tennant first manufactures chlorine-based bleach on a large scale, at the St. Rollox Works, Glasgow

1823   Charles Macintosh, in Glasgow, patents a method of dissolving rubber in naphtha and applying the solution to fabric

1830   Chilean sodium nitrate becomes available in Britain

1841   Charles Goodyear's American patent for vulcanising rubber

1842   John Bennett Lawes patents his process for making superphosphate

1845   Arthur Albright begins to make phosphorus from bone ash
       Royal College of Chemistry founded

1849   Salrother, in Vienna, discovers how to convert the dangerous white phosphorus into the less dangerous red phosphorus

1852   James Crossley Eno, in Newcastle, begins making Eno's Fruit Salt

1856   W. H. Perkin discovers the first commercially successful synthetic dye

1863   Alkali Works Act, controlling pollution of the atmosphere by hydrochloric acid gas

1869   John Hyatt invents celluloid

1873   Ludwig Mond and John Brunner set up a plant at Winnington, Cheshire, to produce soda by the Belgian Solvay process

1888   William Hesketh founds the Port Sunlight soap factory

1907   Leo Baekeland begins production of Bakelite

1909   Karl Hofmann produces a synthetic rubber, Buna rubber

1926   Imperial Chemical Industries formed, by the amalgamation of the United Alkali Co., Brunner, Mond and Co., the British Dyestuffs Corporation and Nobel Industries

1929   Lever Bros. merged with the Dutch margarine firm, Jurgens, to form Unilever

1931 J. A. Nieuwland, in the United States, discovers Neoprene, an improved type of synthetic rubber

Docks and harbours

1698 The first Eddystone lighthouse, designed by Henry Winstanley

1759 John Smeaton's Eddystone lighthouse

1802 West India Docks, London, completed, the first to provide a system of warehousing

1809 William Jessop completes the Cumberland Basin, Bristol, improved by I. K. Brunel in 1848

1824 Jesse Hartley appointed engineer to Liverpool docks and began a programme of extensive development, which included the Albert Dock and its warehouse

1828 St. Katharine's Dock, London, completed, to designs by Thomas Telford

1848 John Rennie's breakwater at Plymouth completed

1880 Royal Albert Dock, London, completed

Electricity

1831 Michael Faraday generates electricity by mechanical means

1866 E. W. von Siemens patents his electro-magnetic generator

*c.***1870** Z. T. Gramme, in Belgium, develops the first practical dynamo

1879 Joseph Swan, in Newcastle, produces incandescent electric lamp

1881 The first public electricity supply, at Godalming, generated by a water wheel

1882 Holborn Viaduct generating station opened, steam-powered

1930 Decision to establish a National Grid for electricity generation in Britain

1948 Nationalisation of electricity generation in Britain

Food and drink

1747 A. S. Margraff, in Germany, discovers that beets and other plants contain sugar

1784 Albion Flour Mills, Blackfriars, powered by Boulton and Watt steam engines

1786 Franz C. Achard establishes his experimental sugar-beet factory, in Germany

1794 Jacob Schweppe, a Swiss, sets up a soft-drink manufactory in Bristol

1814 The egg-shaped glass bottle introduced in Britain

1815 Francois Appert establishes a canning factory in France

1834 Jacob Perkins' patent for a vapour compression mechanical refrigerator, using a hydrocarbon obtained from the destructive distillation of rubber

1853 Gail Borden's American patent for evaporated milk

1858 The screw-topped jar (the Mason jar) invented in the United States by John Landis Mason

1869 First British patent for margarine

1872 Screw-stopper for bottles patented by Henry Barrett

1875 Hiram Codd, of London, patents the glass marble stopper

1876 Carl Linde's ammonia compressor, for industrial refrigeration

1880 First shipload of Australian frozen meat reaches Britain

c.1885 Beginnings of milk-bottling

1890 Milk pasteurisation, based on Louis Pasteur's researches

1892 The crown-cork patented by William Painter, in the United States

c.1905 Development of automatic bottling and jar-filling machinery

Gas

1792 William Murdock lights a room with gas, at Redruth, Cornwall

1812 Gas Light and Coke Co. established; the first to provide a public gas supply

1865 Water-geyser first used

1867 First gas ring

1880 First radiant gas fire

1885 Gas-mantle invented by Carl Auer von Welsbach

Internal combustion engines

1860 Lenoir's gas engine, the first to be made in quantity
1876 Nicolas Otto's four-stroke gas engine
1880 Dugald Clerk's two-stroke engine
1884 Gottlieb Daimler's high-speed petrol engine
1893 Rudolf Diesel's engine

Kiln products – bricks, tiles, pottery, glass

1615 Sir Robert Mansel's patent for making glass with coal
_c._1650 Glass wine-bottles begin to replace leather and earthenware
1687 Bernard Perrot's invention of plate-glass
1695 Glass duty first imposed in Britain. Finally repealed in 1845
1745 Cookworthy begins experiments to make porcelain
1759 Josiah Wedgwood sets up on his own account at Burslem
1767 Coade stone first manufactured
1768 Porcelain manufacture begun at Sèvres.
Cookworthy's first British patent for true porcelain
1773 Cast plate-glass first made in England, at Ravenshead, St. Helens, Lancashire
1784 Introduction of the Brick Tax. Repealed in 1850
1803 Tiles taxed. Repealed in 1833
1832 Lucas Chance brings the cylinder method of sheet-glass making to England from Lorraine
1839 Sir James Chance's patent for grinding and polishing sheet-glass
1840 The Chatsworth Conservatory designed by Joseph Paxton
1841 William Irving invents wire-cutting process for brick-making
1851 Joseph Paxton completes the Crystal Palace
1856 Henry Bessemer's first converter, to produce low-carbon iron
1858 Friedrich Hoffmann patents the continuous kiln
1859 Doultons of Lambeth make the first glazed ceramic kitchen sink
1873 Maws and Craven Dunnill introduce the steam-driven tile-press
1875 First brick-extruding machine, at Bridgwater, Somerset

1879 Thomas and Gilchrist announce their discovery of the basic process for making iron from phosphoric ore

c.1885 Brick-production begins at Fletton, near Peterborough

1898 Pilkingtons pioneer wired-glass

1900 Introduction of glass bricks.
'Glass-silk', i.e. glass-fibre, first made in Germany

1959 Pilkingtons begin making float-glass at St. Helens

Machine tools, machines, instruments

1579 Besson's screw-cutting lathe

1644 William Gascoigne's micrometer

c.1729 Christopher Polhem's hand-operated gear-cutting machine

c.1760 Job and William Wyatt's screw-making machine

1775 Wilkinson's horizontal boring machine for the barrels of cannon

c.1780 Circular saw invented by Walter Taylor, of Southampton

1783 Samuel Réhé's tool and cutter grinder

1786 Ezekiel Reed's American patent for a nail-making machine

c.1800 Machine for planing metal introduced in England, probably by Matthew Murray, of Leeds

1802 Rotary wood-planer built by Joseph Bramah for Woolwich Arsenal

1817 Roberts' improved lathe

1818 Thomas Blanchard's copying-lathe introduced in Massachusetts.
Eli Whitney's invention of the milling machine for producing flat surfaces in metal, in the United States

c.1830 Henry Maudslay's bench micrometer, accurate to .0001 inch

1834 Wheaton's elliptical grinding machine introduced in the United States

1836 First machine for making tongues and grooves in floor boards, using rotary cutter.
James Nasmyth's shaping machine

1839 Nasmyth's steam-hammer

c.1840 Pointed wood-screws made by machine in America

1841 Joseph Whitworth's first standard range of screw threads

1843	Henry Maudslay introduces the all-metal lathe.
	Joseph Whitworth's lathe
1849	First successful bandsaw introduced in the United States
1853	Establishment of the Tangye Works in Birmingham to make hydraulic jacks and other hydraulic equipment
c.1855	Robbins and Laurence turret lathe introduced in the United States
1860	Twist drills introduced in the United States
1861	Automatic screw-making lathe in use in the United States.
	The Brown and Sharpe Company, of Rhode Island, make the first universal milling machine
1868	C. L. Sholes and C. Glidden, of Milwaukee, develop the first successful typewriter, subsequently known as the Remington No. 1
1871	B. C. Tilghman invents sand-blasting, in the United States
1876	Brown and Sharpe's universal grinder
1878	Peter Brotherhood's patent for an air-compressor
1886	J. M. Poole's precision grinding machine introduced in America.
	Osborne Reynold's paper to the Royal Society on the theory of lubrication
1887	F. J. Rowan's portable electric drill
c.1890	Introduction of the Ruston and Dunbar Steam Navvy. Stothert and Pitt, of Bath, design the first travelling steam-crane, for constructing the Admiralty dockyard, Peterhead
1891	E. A. Acheson's American patent for Carborundum, for grinding
1897	E. R. Fellows' American patent for a gear-shaping machine
1899	Pratt and Whitney introduce, in the United States, a machine for grinding the cups and cones of bicycle ball-bearings

Metals

c.1640	Slitting-mills first used, in Sweden
1707	Abraham Darby's patent for dry-sand moulding
1709	Abraham Darby successfully smelts iron-ore with coke

c.1710 Cast-iron railings first used in Britain

c.1742 Benjamin Huntsman's crucible steel process

1751 Nickel first isolated

c.1760 Christopher Polheim invents the three-high rolling mill, in Sweden, but it was not widely adopted for another hundred years

John Smeaton's invention of the cast-iron blowing cylinder

1774 Manganese first isolated

1775 James Watt installs a steam blowing-machine at John Wilkinson's Willey furnaces

1781 Molybdenum first isolated

1784 Henry Cort introduces the iron-puddling process

1794 Titanium first isolated

1797 Chromium first isolated

1820 Thomas Burr's process for extruding seamless lead tubes

1828 James Neilson's invention of hot-blast for pre-heating the air to the blast-furnace

1830 Vanadium first isolated

1850 Aluminium produced in France by chemical electrolysis

1864 Pierre Martin's discovery that scrap iron could be used in the Siemens open-hearth process

1885 Electric arc welding introduced.

Mannesmann process for making steel tubes

1897 First use of aluminium sheet, on the dome of S. Gioacchino, Rome

c.1900 Oxy-acetylene welding first used

1915 Stainless steel discovered

1951 First aluminium aircraft hangar in Britain, at London Airport

Mining

c.1620 Gunpowder first used for blasting in British mines

1784 First steam winding-engine, at Walker Colliery, Tyneside

1814 Davy's safety-lamp

c.1840 The Cornish man-engine, for taking miners up and down shafts.

Iron-wire ropes introduced for pit-winding

***c*.1860** Centrifugal fans used for ventilating coal-mines
1863 Thomas Harrison's coal-cutter, powered by compressed air

Railways, tramways

1802 Trevithick builds the first steam railway locomotive, at Coalbrookdale
1825 Opening of the Stockton and Darlington Railway
1829 George Stephenson's 'Rocket' wins the Rainhill locomotive trials
1830 Inauguration of the Liverpool–Manchester railway
1835 London–Birmingham railway opened, with its London terminus at Chalk Farm. Extended to Euston in 1838
1840 Opening of the London–Southampton line
1841 Opening of the Great Western, Bristol–Paddington
1846 The London and Birmingham line amalgamated with the Grand Junction and the Manchester and Birmingham, to create the London and North-Western Railway
1849 Robert Stephenson's tubular bridge at Conway
1850 Britannia tubular bridge opened, carrying the Chester and Holyhead railway across the Menai Straits
1852 Completion of the Great Northern main line, King's Cross to York
1859 Brunel's Royal Albert Bridge at Saltash opened
1860 First street tramway in Britain, horse-drawn, at Birkenhead
***c*.1875** Westinghouse continuous air-brake for trains in general use
1878 First Tay bridge opened. Collapsed the following year
1879 Use of Mechanical Power on Tramways Act
1883 First electric tramway in Britain, built by Magnus Volk, at Brighton
1884 Completion of the Inner Circle line
1887 Present Tay bridge opened
1890 Forth bridge opened, using mild steel instead of wrought-iron

Roads, road vehicles

1663 First Turnpike Act, 'for repairing the highways within the counties of Hereford, Cambridge and Huntingdon'

1716	Corps des Ponts et Chaussées established, the first body of professional engineers in the world
1767	The first iron rails, cast at Coalbrookdale
1779	The Iron Bridge across the Severn in Shropshire, the first iron bridge in the world
1796	The Wear bridge at Sunderland
1801	Richard Trevithick tests his steam-carriage on a road at Camborne, Cornwall
1803	Thomas Telford appointed to improve and build roads in Scotland
1815	John Loudon McAdam appointed Surveyor-General of the Bristol Roads
1820	Union Chain Bridge, Berwick-on-Tweed, completed, the earliest surviving suspension bridge
1825	Telford completes the suspension bridge over the Menai Straits
c.1830	Asphalt first used for road-surfacing, in France. Tarmac – tar and stones mixed while the tar is hot – first used to surface McAdam roads, in Nottinghamshire
1850	First concrete roads, in Austria
1861	Cranks and pedals first used on a bicycle
1868	Edward Cowper's patent for a wire-spoked tension wheel
1879	Renold invents modern type of bushed roller chain, for bicycles
1885	Rover safety-bicycle
1888	First successful pneumatic tyres, patented by J. B. Dunlop
1900	Frederick Lanchester founds his works in Birmingham
1908	The first Model T Ford

Shipbuilding, shipping

1787	The first iron boat, launched by John Wilkinson into the Severn at Coalbrookdale
1789	Symington tests his steam-propelled boat on the Forth–Clyde Canal
1802	Test of the steam paddle tug, 'Charlotte Dundas', on the Forth–Clyde Canal
1819	The first steamship to enter regular sea-going service, the 'Rob Roy', built by William Denny of Dumbarton

1822	The 'Aaron Manby', the first iron steamship to put to sea, on a voyage from London to Rouen
1837	Brunel's 'Great Western' (1340 tons) the first true Atlantic steamship
1838	Launch of the 'Archimedes', the first successful screw-steamer
1845	Brunel's 'Great Britain' (3400 tons)
1859	Brunel's 'Great Eastern' (21 000 tons)
1867	John McFarlane Gray's steam-powered steering gear
1872	William and Robert Froude's experimental tank for testing ship-models
1896	Charles Parsons builds the 'Turbinia', the first ship in the world to be propelled by turbines

Steam

1698	Thomas Savery's patent for 'raising water by the impellent force of fire'
1710	Thomas Newcomen's first steam engine, at Huel Vor tin-mine; it was a failure
1712	The first successful Newcomen engine demonstrated, at Dudley Castle, Staffordshire
1769	James Watt's patent for a separate condenser
1845	Sir William Fairbairn patents the Lancashire boiler
1849	G. H. Corliss, in the United States, patents his valve-gear for steam engines
1867	G. H. Babcock and S. Wilcox patent, in the United States, the first successful water-tube boiler
1884	Sir Charles Parsons' steam turbine

Stone

1727	Avon Navigation completed, allowing Bath stone to be sent by barge to Bristol, and then by ship to London and elsewhere
c.1800	Feather and tare method of splitting granite introduced
1839–40	Box tunnel on GWR reveals enormous quantities of Bath stone
1887	Bath Stone Firms Ltd. established
1899	Bath Stone Firms take over the Portland quarries. In 1911 the name was changed to the Bath and Portland Stone Firms Ltd.

Telephones, radio, television, telegraph, postal services

1839 First electric telegraph in Britain, Paddington–West Drayton

1840 Penny post introduced by Rowland Hill

1846 Foundation of the Electric Telegraph Co. in Britain

1851 Submarine cable between England and France

1866 The first successful Atlantic cable, from Valentia, Ireland, to Newfoundland

1879 First British telephone exchange, in London

1896 G. Marconi's first wireless patent, for the transmission of signals, not words

1901 Wireless signals from Cornwall received in Newfoundland

1902 In Pittsburgh, R. A. Fessenden first uses wireless waves to carry the human voice

1906 Lee de Forest, in the United States, makes the first triode valve.
In London, J. A. Fleming experiments with the first thermionic diode valve

1912 GPO acquires all private telephone systems in Britain, except in Hull

1920 Opening of KDKA, Pittsburgh, the first public broadcasting station in the world

1926 J. L. Baird demonstrates television

*c.***1950** Subscriber-dialling introduced in Britain

Textiles

*c.***1590** William Lee invents the knitting-frame

1702 Thomas Cotchett's silk-spinning mill at Derby pioneers the factory system

1733 John Kay's flying shuttle

1738 Lewis Paul and John Wyatt file their patent for a roller-drawing machine to mechanise spinning

1758 Jedediah Strutt's patent for a rib-knitting machine

*c.***1760** James Hargreaves' jenny, for spinning cotton on multiple spindles

*c.***1770** Richard Arkwright's water-frame, for mechanising spinning

1775 J. Crane and J. Tarrett, in Nottinghamshire, independently invent a warp-knitting machine

1779	Samuel Crompton's spinning-mule, a combination of the jenny and the water-frame
1784	Edmund Cartwright's power-loom
c.1800	Jacquard system of controlling weaving by punched cards first used in Britain
1809	John Heathcoat's machine for imitating hand-made pillow lace
1813	Horrocks' improved power-loom. John Lever adapts Heathcoat's machine to make patterned lace
1828	John Thorp's invention of the ring-spinning water-frame, in the United States
1884	Hilaire de Chardonnet patents rayon
1885	Schutzenberger patents Celanese
1939	Du Pont patents Nylon

Water, sewage, refuse-disposal

1582	Peter Morice's water-powered pumping-station at London Bridge, giving the city its first regular supply of pumped water from the Thames
1613	Sir Hugh Myddelton's New River, bringing fresh water from Hertfordshire to London
1829	The first sand filter beds, invented by James Simpson, engineer to the Chelsea Water Company
1833	London's first refuse destructor, at Ealing
1855	Metropolitan Board of Works established, to provide an efficient sewerage system for London and prevent pollution of the Thames

Water-power, wind-power

1722	Meike's spring-sail
1789	Hooper's roller-blind sail
1796	Joseph Bramah's patent for an hydraulic press
1797	J. M. Montgolfier's hydraulic ram-pump
1807	The 'patent-sail', with automatic sail-control
1818	The Massachusetts centrifugal pump introduced in America
1824	Benoît Fourneyron's water-turbine
1913	Kaplan's turbine patented, in Sweden

Waterways

1488   Pound lock in use near Padua

1497   Leonardo da Vinci built six pound locks near Milan

1563   John Trew began work on the Exeter Canal

1618   John Gilbert's patent for a dredger

1742   Completion of the Newry Canal, in Ireland

1760   Completion of the Sankey Brook Canal, from the Mersey to St. Helens

1761   Completion of the Bridgewater Canal, designed by James Brindley, from Worsley Colliery to Manchester and including the first canal aqueduct, the Barton aqueduct (demolished in 1893)

1772   Opening of James Brindley's Wolverhampton, later called the Stafford and Worcester, Canal, completing the Grand Trunk link between the Mersey, Humber and Severn

1777   Completion of James Brindley's Trent and Mersey Canal, as part of the Grand Trunk

1787   Opening of Forth–Clyde Canal, engineered by John Smeaton

1796   Telford's iron canal aqueduct, at Longdon-on-Tern, Shropshire, the first in the world

1801   Completion of Telford's cast-iron Chirk aqueduct

1805   Completion of Telford's cast-iron aqueduct at Pont Cysyllte

1822   Opening of Telford's Caledonian Canal

1890   Opening of the Manchester Ship Canal, the most highly mechanised civil engineering project of the nineteenth century

Wood products

1767   Wind-driven sawmill in Limehouse destroyed by hand-sawyers

1844   Plywood used for chair-seats, at Revel, Esthonia

c.1870 Kiln-drying of timber introduced

c.1890 Knife-cutting machines allowed production of large sheets of plywood veneers

1909   D. M. Sutherland begins to produce pulpboard at his factory at Sunbury-on-Thames

1945   Chip-board used commercially

Workers' housing

1851 Titus Salt begins construction of Saltaire, near Bradford

1864 The Peabody Trust's first tenements, at Spitalfields, London

1888 First houses constructed at Port Sunlight

1895 Bournville begun

1926 Stewartby begun, to house workers from the adjacent brickworks

Index

*Note that Sections Four, Five and Six of the text are
compiled on an alphabetical basis.*